World Parliament
of Religions
August 30, 1993

Dear Rosamund,

What a nice occasion to share lunch, ideas, experiences.

Blessings to you

Rudi

*imagine...
a new bible*

ABOUT THE AUTHOR

Rudi Gelsey was born in Vienna, Austria, in 1926 and came to North America in 1949. He holds a graduate degree in political science from the University of Geneva, Switzerland, and has a bachelor in divinity from the University of Chicago. The Reverend Rudi Gelsey had pastorates in South Bend, Philadelphia and Westchester County, N.Y. Since 1973, he is the minister of the First Unitarian-Universalist Church of Detroit. He is listed in *Who's Who in Religion* and has been active in the peace movement, civil rights, community organization and humanistic psychology. He is married to Getrud Linsenmair and has three children, Florence, Andrew and Alex.

CONTENTS

ACKNOWLEDGMENTS 11
FOREWORD 13

Chapter One
GENESIS
    Prologue: In The Beginning, Chaos 17
1. The Seven Days Of Creation 18
2. Adam And Eve: Is Paradise Lost Forever? .. 19
3. Brotherly Affection: Cain And Abel 20
4. Salvation From Calamities:
    The Ark Of Noah And Nehaya 21
5. The Power To Understand:
    The Tower Of Babel 23

Chapter Two
HISTORY IN THE MAKING
    Prologue: God's Covenant:
    Let There Be Peace 25
1. The Promised Land: God And Abraham ... 26
2. Human Conscience Triumphant:
    Saving Isaac 27
3. Accepting Differences:
    Isaac And Ishmael 28
4. All Of God's Children Are Equal.
    Jacob And Esau 28
5. Here Comes Joseph, The Dreamer 30

Chapter Three
FROM SLAVERY TO FREEDOM
    Prologue: Liberty For All 35

1. No Need To Explain:
   "I Am Who I Am" 36
2. On Behalf Of The Oppressed:
   "Let My People Go" 38
3. Path To Freedom:
   Wandering In The Wilderness 39
4. Temptation: The Golden Calf............ 41
5. Moses: "I Have Been To The Mountain Top" 41

Chapter Four
PEACE IS THE WAY
   Prologue: Modeling War Or Peace 43
1. Joshua's Unholy War.................. 44
2. Gideon:
   Deliverer From The Scourge Of War 46
3. Love Conquers All:
   Samson And Delilah 49
4. Reconciliation: David And Goliath 51
5. Judith: Heroine For Peace 53

Chapter Five
THE GLORY AND PITY OF RULERS
   Prologue:
   The Price Of Power and Powerlessness 57
1. From Samuel The Priest
   To Saul The King..................... 59
2. David:
   Humble Shepherd, Mighty Conqueror 61
3. Pearls Of Wisdom, Outrageous Wealth:
   King Solomon 65

Chapter Six
PROPHETS OF WOE AND SALVATION
   Prologue: Messengers of God............ 67
1. First Isaiah:
   The Wolf Shall Dwell With The Lamb 69
2. Make Straight A Highway For Peace:
   Second Isaiah 72

3. Third Isaiah:
   I Create A New Heaven And Earth   73
4. Jeremiah:
   Death Will Seem Preferable To Life   74
5. Ezekiel:
   In The Valley Of Dry Bones And Exile   78
6. Amos: Let Justice Flow Like Water   78
7. Micah: What Does Life Require Of Thee? . . .   80

Chapter Seven
OF LIFE AND DEATH
   Prologue: Perennial Stories   81
1. Job Answers God   83
2. Jonah And The Whale:
   A Tale Of Forgiveness   91
3. Esther: Averting Destruction   93
4. Ecclesiastes: Beyond Vanity, Meaning   97
5. Daniel: Endtime—Judgment Or Joy   99

Chapter Eight
EXILE AND RETURN
   Prologue: The Road Less Traveled 101
1. Exile:
   How Shall We Sing In A Foreign Land? 102
2. There Shall Not Be Another Masada 106
3. Two Millenia Of Persecutions:
   What Next? 111
4. The Mystery And Message Of Auschwitz . . . 117
5. Return To Israel 119

EPILOGUE
   You Can Go Home Again 125

ACKNOWLEDGMENTS

Grateful acknowledgment is made by the author for use of passages from:

1. Max Dimont. *Jews, God and History,* New York: Simon and Schuster, 1962.
2. Elie Wiesel. *One Generation After,* New York: Random House, 1970.
3. Abraham Joshua Heschel. *Israel, an Echo of Eternity,* New York: Farrar, Straus and Giroux, 1967

Reprinted by permission.

imagine... a new bible

The Reverend Rudi Gelsey

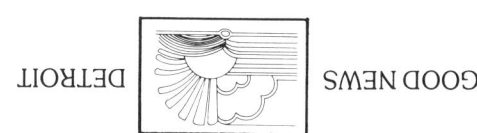

GOOD NEWS — DETROIT

Copyright © 1982 by Rudolf C. Gelsey

All rights reserved

Published by:
THE GOOD NEWS PUBLISHING COMPANY
16541 Warwick
Detroit, Michigan 48219

Cover and jacket design by:
INNOVATIONS GRAPHIC DESIGN

ISBN—Hard: 0-9608562-0-x
ISBN—Soft: 0-9608562-1-8

Printed by Harlo Press, 50 Victor, Detroit, Michigan 48203

"Far from being a mere relic of ancient literature, the Bible in our lives is living power, radiating anticipations. Not a document sealed and finished. It is a book alive that goes on and extends into the present—always being written, always disclosing and unfolding. We are in labor with Biblical visions."

—Abraham Joshua Heschel

FOREWORD

In the past, the Bible has seen dozens of new translations and thousands of commentaries. What is required is not another stylistic update or clever reinterpretation. Out of the rich lore of Biblical times and the depths of the collective unconscious, let us dream new visions to help invent a future of human cooperation.

The stories of the Old and New Testament are fountainheads of our cultural and religious heritage, yet the Bible, like television, contains a great deal of violence. Blood-curdling plagues upon Egypt and the genocidal conquest of the land of Canaan typify a lust to annihilate and fascination with death which need to be replaced with the art of peaceful problem-solving.

The Scriptures, reflecting the mores of patriarchal times are sexist, at least by today's standards. Biblical stories see Eve as a temptress, Delilah as a traitor. Of Noah's wife it could be said, "Nobody knows her name."

We deplore sibling rivalry? Its archetypes, found in tales such as Jacob and Esau, make it appear that competition is the nature of reality.

There is a need for creative mythology; new endings for old stories. What if God and parents played no favorites, encouraging Cain and Abel to be truly brothers? Are we willing to conceive a scenario where Adam and Eve are not expelled from Paradise forever? Imagine God's covenant with Abraham having to do with peace rather than circumcision! Think of the Tower of Babel as a center for learning and mutual understanding.

Objection! That is not how it happened. Actually, the Bible reflects the insights and social customs of other millenia in distant lands. If the Bible were written today, chances are Biblical authors would take different directions. Even in those faraway days, the Bible was not uniform in its outlook and had two creation stories in the Book of Genesis. If there was room for alternate understandings then, why not a new version based on more advanced knowledge available nowadays?

Many people like the fury and glory of the original. Would positive outcomes not drain the Bible of dramatic tension?

The trouble with the human quest for the excitement of battle and bloodshed is that thoughtful, peaceful solutions to conflicts are imperative in this nuclear age. Heroic values may have been a critical survival skill for ancient Israelites. If Armageddon is to be cancelled, we need to develop moral and psychological equivalents to the satisfactions many people derive from aggressive drives.

Using the framework of age-old stories, this is an alternative storybook of Biblical characters and episodes, inviting the reader to hear good news for the modern world.

imagine...
a new bible

CHAPTER ONE
GENESIS

Prologue: In the Beginning, Chaos

"In the beginning, God" is the resplendent opening of the Old Testament, a vision that has inspired countless generations. Why should anyone wish to tamper with this glorious perspective? The reason is that it puts perfection, power and meaning at the outset of creation with a descending spiral thereafter. Following the first seven days of creation, there is, in quick succession, the sinning of Adam and Eve; their expulsion from Paradise; murder and fratricide; God repents of having created the world and sends a devastating flood, with the ark of Noah as a saving remnant. To complete the dismal picture, God punishes humankind at the Tower of Babel with a confusion of tongues.

After extolling to high heaven the original act of creation, a dramatic series of catastrophic developments ensue. "In the beginning, chaos" would seem better to reflect the nature of our origins.

Descending from divine order and perfection to human sin and imperfection encourages guilt and despair. Humanity is offered paradise and we miss it. If, by contrast, the world is seen as a progression from barren lifelessness to luscious plant, animal and human life, an ascending evolutionary thrust invites hopefulness. Instead of being expelled from the Garden of Eden, we are propelled toward a higher human consciousness. Sin, murder, destruction, confusion are no more our ominous destiny. Human cooperation, peace and love can become the directions in which we move. It has been said of old that in the beginning there was God and perfect harmony. Actually, in the beginning there was chaos and imperfection. Our task now is to fulfill our human and divine potential.

1.
The Seven Days of Creation

In the beginning, chaos. The universe was without form; an immense void with neither spirit, meaning, life nor purpose, and darkness was upon the face of the deep.

Out of primeval chaos, in ways still mysterious to the human mind, energy, heat and radiation erupted into existence. The universe came into being, dividing emptiness from form. It was the beginning of some principle of order: the first day of creation.

Gradually, the intense heat cooled off, allowing atoms to form and survive. The dense fog cleared; the universe became transparent. There were atoms and light: the second day of creation.

At first, small particles whirled in solitude through the immensities of empty space. Eventually, atoms began to coalesce with others, stars and galaxies were formed: the third day of creation.

As an atmosphere enveloped the planet earth, inanimate matter evolved into living cells, without being destroyed by radiation. Life began in the oceans and lakes. The energy from the sun and aeons of time brought the formation of organic molecules. Plants appeared in water and soil: the fourth day of creation.

As the earth was covered with grass and trees, flowers and fruit, life became more and more complex. Instead of being merely anchored in water or rooted in the soil, living things started to move, fish swimming in the waters, animals creeping on the earth, birds flying in the sky: the fifth day of creation.

The animal kingdom and plants express a great richness and variety, yet it is with humankind that nature became self-conscious. Man and woman emerged on earth: the sixth day of creation.

As the universe arose, out of chaos and darkness into order and light, behold the creative process was good.

Yet, amid the progressive evolution from primordial void to human consciousness, the original principles still remained strong. The universe comprises black holes. Upon the planet earth, humankind has exploited nature, caused pollution, waged war, practiced slavery, tyranny and discrimination.

And now the time is upon us to covenant with the universe, life and one another to acknowledge the earth as a sacred trust. As order, spirit and meaning come into the universe and into our lives, humanity embarks upon the final stage of evolutionary ascent: the seventh day of creation.

2.
Adam and Eve: Is Paradise Lost Forever?

God planted a garden in Eden and placed there the first man, Adam, and the first woman, Eve. God caused to spring up from the soil every kind of vegetation beautiful to behold, with a tree of life in the middle of the garden.

And God spoke to Adam and Eve: "Creation is yours to enjoy, a pleasure to the eyes and palate. I entrust you with a magnificent planet sailing safely in space. During the day, the sun will give you warmth and light; at night the moon will be a companion and the stars will shine in the firmament as a symbol of my eternal care and presence. I give you a pleasant dwelling place; keep it that way. In the middle of the Garden of Eden, I have planted a magnificent tree full of majesty. Under its branches there is rest, peace and harmony. Consider this as holy ground. Approach it with awe and thanksgiving, as a symbol of all creation. You are my stewards on earth where life blooms in infinite richness. Be helpful to one another and you will enjoy the Garden of Eden for time immemorial."

Adam and Eve had all of Paradise available to them, fruit from the trees, vegetables from the soil and water from pure springs. Yet, somehow man and woman wanted more. Instead of worshiping in gratitude at the tree of life, they decided to cut it down and use it for wood.

God was sad and angry that for Adam and Eve, enough was not enough. Greed can become an all-consuming passion and the Divine Spirit was tempted to banish humankind from Paradise forever, punishing men with hard labor and women with painful childbirth. Though disappointed, God decided not to give in to the first impulse of vengeance. "Let me not expect perfection from Adam and Eve, but grant the human species another chance. Whenever a newborn child enters the light of the world, Paradise continues to be its divine birthright. The Garden of Eden is not a location, it is a state of mind. Sometimes the spirit of goodwill, happiness, cooperation and serenity prevails, and Paradise dwells in the heart. At other times greed, hatred and jealousy rear their ugly heads and Paradise is lost for the time being, only to be reborn with every generation as the eternal promise of my infinite, unconditional love."

3.
Brotherly Affection: Cain and Abel

Adam and Eve loved each other. Eve conceived and gave birth to Cain, a beautiful infant, extending the human family from man and woman to parents and child. Adam and Eve bestowed tender loving care, rejoiced over their first-born baby and, within a short time, a second child, Abel, was born.

Cain had been the center of his parents' attention. Now he had to share Adam and Eve with Abel. However, Cain soon realized that he was not loved less, only longer. The brothers became playmates and friends, enjoyed being together and helped one another. When grown men, Abel kept the flocks, while Cain tilled the soil.

Time passed and Cain brought some of the produce of the soil as an offering to God, while Abel sacrificed the first-born of his flock. God looked with favor on both gifts and appreciated their diverse and equally meaningful acts of devotion.

Abel and Cain were happy that neither God nor parents played favorites. The brothers supported each other in all difficulties, knowing deep down that each sibling is the other sibling's keeper. Each person does well to care for self, fellow human beings, and all of Creation. God is love, warmth and protection, and people are made in the image of God.

4.
Salvation From Calamities:
The Ark of Noah and Nehaya

Ages ago, when the earth was young, there were many natural catastrophes like sudden earthquakes, volcanic explosions, massive floods. The planet needed time to become stable.

Eventually people began to feel safe. When Noah and Nehaya lived, a few generations after Adam and Eve, survival had become more or less taken for granted. In the memory of the oldest men and women, there was no recollection of a major natural calamity. Individuals did not live any more in perpetual fear of imminent destruction. As nature appeared less threatening, people began to think they were in charge of their environment.

Somehow, Noah was not that self-confident. As he watched thunder, lightning and downpours of rain, he wondered, "Suppose the sluices of the heavens open up and keep going for months on end. What if there is an all-engulfing flood and everyone perishes in the waters?"

One night Noah dreamed of just such a disaster. He

woke in a state of panic. In his nightmare, Noah had seen humans and animals in a hellish scene of onrushing waters, people vainly clinging to trees and tents.

Noah was not sure what to make of it, so he spoke about the dream to his wife, Nehaya and some neighbors. Noah's friends made light of the vision, "The rains always stop, the rainbow and the sun return; there is nothing to fear." Nehaya, on the other hand, knew that her husband was neither a wild seer nor a coward. She was mindful that in some instances Noah's dreams had predicted a future event. "Do you think there is any way in which we could take measures of precaution, like moving from the valley to a higher plateau?" Nehaya asked.

Noah's intuition was that the problem did not yield to such a relatively easy answer. Confused and frightened, Noah pondered on what to do next.

The following night, Noah saw the vision of a huge ship, around it people drowning, while Noah, Nehaya and their families, along with some animals in pairs, were gathered on board and survived the flood.

Noah threw all hesitations to the wind and decided to heed the message. "What I need is to prepare myself against a potential disaster. Let us build an ark for our safety, make it big enough to hold family, friends and animals, enough food to last during an emergency." Nehaya thought these were extreme measures, yet she trusted Noah's judgment.

Neighbors were less sympathetic and ridiculed him, especially on a beautiful day of balmy sunshine, when Noah and family started to gather gopher wood for the building of the ark. Noah and Nehaya were not to be deterred, and for several months labored mightily to complete the ship. "If my dream was wrong," Noah thought, "so much the better; yet, if it was true, I will be prepared. At stake is my personal survival, as well as the continuation of the human race. I care about *humanity and the animal kingdom. If some precautions can save us from extinction, then so be it."*

About a week after Noah, Nehaya and helpers completed their ark, the heavens opened up, rains came, rivers rose out of their beds, and even the high hills became submerged. All that had lived on the dry land died, except Noah, Nehaya, their sons and the sons' wives, along with good friends, as well as two beasts; one male and one female of every species, all of whom found refuge upon the ark.

The flood raged on day after day. It seemed as if the waters that covered the earth would never recede, and supplies on the ark started to run low.

After five weeks of turbulence, Noah and Nehaya became increasingly depressed. In all this time, there had not been a day of sunshine, only sullen skies and destruction; they also missed neighbors who had perished in the flood.

Finally, the downpour ended. Winds began to dry up the landscape. At the end of forty days Noah and Nehaya sent forth a dove to see how much the waters had receded. The dove found no rest for her feet, so she returned to the ark.

After another seven days, the couple lowered the bird once more, and this time she came back with an olive branch in her beak. Thus, Noah and Nehaya knew that the waters were abating. Following another week, they sent out the dove again, and this time the bird did not return, for she had found dry earth. Soon thereafter, the ark ran aground and everyone disembarked to start a new life out of the ruins of the old

As Noah and Nehaya stepped off the ark, and saw the desolation, they grieved over so much destruction in the wake of the flood. They offered a prayer for the souls of all who had perished and proceeded to give thanks to whatever powers that be for a marvelous deliverance. They were grateful for Noah's dream and their own willingness to listen to the inspiration which had guided them in these difficult times. They rejoiced *that people and animals had not been entirely wiped off the face of the earth, and had another chance to live and laugh and love.*

5.
The Power to Understand: The Tower of Babel

After the flood was over, and Nehaya's family had survived, humankind was fruitful, multiplied and replenished the earth. People settled East and West, North and South. Living in different parts of the world, and lacking contact with one another, they began to speak different languages, and it became more difficult for people to understand distant neighbors. While the roar of the lion is the same in Africa and Asia, and the twitter of a sparrow identical in Europe and America, human beings developed their own distinctive tongues that made communication difficult.

To help overcome their barriers, the inhabitants of Chaldea decided to build a high tower that could be seen from afar and named it the Tower of Babel. The intent was to have an academy of learning where people from all over would come together to school themselves in the art of mutual understanding. This meant to study each other's language, learn skills of relating and caring about far-flung fellow humans. While geographically people lived in remote regions, there would always be a center where that which binds humans together is studied, practiced and nurtured. And so, beyond all superficial differences, the Tower of Babel stands like a beacon for the unity of humankind.

CHAPTER TWO
HISTORY IN THE MAKING

Prologue: God's Covenant: Let There Be Peace

According to the Old Testament, God entered a covenant with Abraham. If all male Israelites submitted to circumcision, God would make the descendants of Abraham his chosen people and give them the fertile crescent of Canaan as the promised land where they could settle. Circumcision is hardly an inspiring symbol for God's covenant. Why would it be of such special, cosmic importance?

As I look back on the history of these past millenia, the central unresolved problem that has plagued humankind is the intolerance, strife, violence and warfare between different tribes, nations, empires, religions. Peace would seem a worthy goal for a divinely inspired world. It makes sense for God's covenant to be shalom, salaam. Circumcision pales into insignificance by comparison with the crucial survival issue of war and peace.

An example of how Biblical history symbolically acts out and perpetuates the age-old enmity between Egypt and Israel is found in the story of Ishmael and Isaac. Ishmael, son of Abraham and an Egyptian bondswoman, is rejected and driven outside the family fold. Isaac, the legitimate Israelite offspring of Abraham and Sarah, is upheld. Ishmael, and Egypt that he represents, are made less acceptable in the eyes of Israel and its God. Biblical mythology here serves the goal of justifying continued hostility. Creative mythology can reverse this unfortunate direction.

Similarly, in the story of Jacob and Esau, Isaac has only one blessing for one son, which breeds jealousy, competition and conflict over the birthright of the first-born. Replacing the paternal blessing with a parental one upon both children, the tension is resolved and brotherhood encouraged.

In the story of God demanding of Abraham to sacrifice his son, Isaac, the basic issue is whether Abraham is willing to be totally obedient to God. The Biblical authors view such unconditional subservience as the highest form of morality. A more contemporary approach is to favor the highest human conscience as the center of meaningful, ethical decision-making. The divine manifests itself not in outside authority, but in the depths of the human soul.

Vengeance and harboring resentment poison the well-springs of human accommodation. Joseph's generous spirit of forgiveness rounds out the attitude necessary for peaceful relations.

1.
The Promised Land: God and Abraham

Back in the mists of prehistory, about two thousand years before the common era, there lived in the city of Haran in ancient Mesopotamia a man named Abraham. Many facts about his life are shrouded in mystery. Some believe that he led caravans of donkeys, carrying goods between his town and distant lands. Others think Abraham was a shepherd who moved around in the nomadic fashion of the times to find grazing grounds for flocks of sheep. However that may be, Abraham was often on the move and, as part of these wanderings, became acquainted with the land of Canaan, Egypt and their fertile crescents.

Abraham was particularly enchanted with Canaan and thought that on the next trip he would bring along his whole family and other members of the tribe. To settle in a new land was a major undertaking full of dangers and there were some doubts and rumblings. "If we leave behind our tents in Mesopotamia, what guarantee is there that we can return?"

Abraham weighed the advantages and disadvantages of settling in the new land, so much so that he even dreamed about it. One night Abraham had an overwhelming vision of God speaking to him. "I will make a covenant with you and your descendants. You shall become the father of a multitude of tribes and nations. I give you the land of Canaan, I will be your God and you will be my people. In return, you are to be peaceful in dealings with other tribes, nations and religions. Live in the spirit of justice and wisdom, harmony with nature, concord with one another and neighbors. Throughout the earth, I have seen countries at war and parents at odds with their offspring. I shall make you my chosen people to teach the world the ways of peace and goodwill."

Abraham fell to his knees, answering: "You have called me, oh God, I am here. With your help I will lead my people to the promised land."

When Abraham awoke, he was filled with a sense of divine guidance and mission. He knew deep in his heart that the time had come for him, the family and tribe to venture forth into the land of Canaan and become an instrument for peace.

2.
Human Conscience Triumphant: Saving Isaac

Abraham and Sarah had a son whom they named Isaac and loved dearly. One night, God sent a messenger ordering Abraham to offer Isaac as a sacrifice to God. Abraham was deeply upset.

Abraham knew of the prevalent custom to offer fruits of the soil and even animals as a divine tribute. He accepted the idea of an agricultural offering and strongly disliked the practice of an animal sacrifice. When it came to the customs found in the worship of Baal and other religions, to kill a first-born child in honor of God, the practice seemed cruel and barbarous, beyond the pale of civilized people.

Abraham wondered what to do. Would God be

angry if divine promptings were disobeyed? He decided to speak about it to Sarah, who was as horrified as Abraham had been. *"I worship a God of love with all my mind, heart and strength. But what gracious God would ask parents to kill a son as an act of gratitude or obedience? I will not consent to such a monstrous deed as murdering our beloved Isaac."* The logic of Sarah's reasoning was compelling. Her feelings of outrage confirmed Abraham's aversion against offering Isaac as a sacrifice.

The following night, Abraham had a dream. In it, he heard God saying, *"I am well pleased with your decision and Sarah's. I wanted to put your conscience to a test. You trusted yourselves and that is good. I bless you for living up to your own highest conscience."* In the morning, Abraham told Sarah of the dream and, as tears of joy streamed down their cheeks, Abraham, Sarah, and Isaac embraced.

3.
Accepting Differences: Isaac and Ishmael

Abraham was married to Sarah who was without child. In those days, it was a reproach against her. Abraham, too, was downcast, having expected to be the father of multitudes. How come that God had promised the land of Canaan to Abraham and his descendants, while spouse Sarah was seemingly unable to bear children? Was it God's will for Abraham to find another wife?

Sarah and Abraham were good friends, unwilling to separate or divorce, so they thought of another way. The couple would continue to live together, yet Abraham would have a child with their Egyptian maid, Hagar. The son who issued from this union was called Ishmael. Even though Sarah had agreed in advance to the arrangement, when it happened she was harsh with Hagar and Ishmael. Eventually, Sarah stopped her resentment and Ishmael grew up harmoniously in the family circle, as if he had been the offspring of Sarah and Abraham. Once Sarah relaxed, she was able to conceive and bear a son, Isaac. Ishmael and Isaac grew up like real brothers and were equally loved by Sarah and Abraham. They were different: Ishmael had Egyptian blood in his veins while Isaac was of Israelite stock. Yet, they cared about each other and lived in harmony and peace, inviting succeeding generations to do likewise.

4.
All of God's Children Are Equal: Jacob and Esau

Jacob and Esau were twins born to Rebecca and Isaac. Esau was the first-born son which, under Hebrew custom, gave him special privileges, responsibilities and blessings. As Jacob grew up, he became increasingly upset that because his brother had been born just moments ahead of him, Esau would hold a superior position in the family. Jacob felt hurt and, as the years went by, was competing with Esau, rather than enjoying his company. Another aspect bothered Jacob. Under existing custom there would be more discrimination against sisters, for they would have second-class status, even if first-born. As a boy, Jacob was disadvantaged by an accident of timing. Had he been a girl, she would have been disinherited altogether. An embittered Jacob wondered how to change the situation.

When it was time for Esau and Jacob to choose an occupation, Esau became a hunter and endeared himself to his father, Isaac, by preparing delicious venison for him. Jacob tilled the soil, reaped the fruits of the earth and was Rebecca's favorite.

One day, Esau, coming from a strenuous hunt, took sick. He was too exhausted and feverish to prepare a meal, so he asked Jacob to give him a portion of pottage. Esau was faint and at his brother's mercy.

Jacob's urge was to get even. For all those years, he had suffered from not being an equal. Now he could get ahead of Esau by asking him to sell his birthright for a bowl of soup.

Once the thought had crossed his mind, Jacob dismissed it. That would be taking undue advantage of a sick brother in need. The competition and bad feelings would continue, only this time it would be Esau's turn to be frustrated. So Jacob gave hot soup to his brother and nurtured him back to health as a matter of simple goodwill.

It came to pass that Isaac and Rebecca had grown old and before dying, called Esau to give him the parental blessing. Esau hurried to the deathbed and remembering how Jacob had saved his life, said to father and mother: "I know it is the custom for a parent only to bless the first-born son; yet were it not for Jacob, I might not be alive today and would have lost my birthright. Allow me to call Jacob, and will you give your joint blessing to both of us?" Moved by Esau's plea, Rebecca said,

"God give ye of the dew of Heaven,
Of the richness of the earth,
Of the joy of the heart."
And Isaac added,
"God continue to grant thee a spirit of brotherly love,
And bless thee abundantly from generation to generation."

Shortly thereafter, Isaac and Rebecca died peacefully.

Jacob and Esau kneeled down to offer thanks for their parents' lives and a prayer of aspiration for their eternal souls. Moved to tears, the brothers embraced each other, enriched by the parental blessing and mutual affection.

5.
Here Comes Joseph, The Dreamer

Joseph, one of Jacob's twelve sons, was a dreamer who had a marvelous ability to understand the hidden meanings of dreams; his own and those of others. His creative imagination endeared him to Jacob. Meanwhile, Joseph was resented by all eleven brothers for being the father's favorite.

One day Joseph told his siblings of a dream. "I saw the sun, moon and eleven stars bowing to me," which was understood as, "Someday, father, mother and the eleven brothers will bow to the ground before Joseph."

This was one more blow for the self-esteem of the brothers, and they began to plot on how to do away with Joseph. One day while they stood near a well, Joseph was seen approaching and the siblings said to each other, "Here comes the dreamer. Let us slay him, throw him into the well, and say that he was devoured by a wild beast. Then we shall see what becomes of his dreams."

No sooner said than done. They seized Joseph by his beautiful, multicolored shepherd coat, pulled it off and threw Joseph into the deep well. The brothers were perplexed as to what to do next. If they assisted Joseph to climb out of the well, he might tell on them. If left there unharmed, Joseph might scream for help and the eleven would still be in trouble.

While they pondered these alternatives, a caravan of Ishmaelites on the way to Egypt passed by. The brothers quickly decided upon a course of action: "Let us sell Joseph to them and never have to put up with him any more; Joseph will be hundreds of miles away. We will not need to fear revenge; his blood will not cry out against us."

Joseph was sold to the Ishmaelites for twenty pieces of silver and taken to far-away Egypt. Meanwhile, the brothers dipped Joseph's tattered coat in the blood of a slaughtered animal and brought it to their father. "Oh merciful God, what a calamity!" Jacob exclaimed, "It is my son's coat. Joseph must have fallen prey to some wild beast." And the father wept for Joseph, put on sackcloth and mourned for a long time.

Meanwhile, in Egypt, Joseph was sold to Potiphar,

one of Pharaoh's officials and commander of the guard. Joseph's qualities were much appreciated by this Egyptian master. Eventually Joseph became a personal attendant in charge of the household and possessions. So when Pharaoh had a dream that no one understood, neither the court magicians nor the wise men of the land, Joseph was summoned to hear the vision which went like this:

"Pharaoh is standing by the Nile. Coming up from the river are seven cows, sleek and fat, which begin to feed among the rushes. Seven other cows, ugly and lean, come out of the Nile and eat the seven sleek and fat ones. Also, growing on one stalk are seven ears of corn, full and ripe. Sprouting after them come seven more, meager and scorched by the east wind. The scanty ears of corn swallow the seven full and ripe ones."

Joseph spoke: "The seven sleek and fat cows, along with the seven ears of ripe corn, are seven years of plentiful harvest. The gaunt and lean cows, along with the withered and meager ears of corn, are seven years of famine that will follow upon the bountiful harvest. The dream is a warning to stock up grain during times of plenty as a reserve for the period of affliction, so that the land and its people will not be destroyed by famine."

Pharaoh admired the clarity of Joseph's insight and decided to make him governor of Egypt.

Joseph ordered that corn be set aside during the years of plenty. After the fruitful years, the tide turned and Egypt's corn fields became desolate. The country would have known mass starvation were it not for Joseph's foresight and his ability to release food from the granaries stocked up during the previous years.

Besides Egypt, Canaan also experienced meager harvests, and when it became known that the land of the pharaohs had grain reserves, many Israelites traveled to Egypt to buy food. Among them were Joseph's brothers. They came before Joseph, who was in charge of grain sales. Despite the long years of separation and the change of circumstances, the brothers recognized each other instantly. Joseph's brothers were joyful and afraid; joyful because of the reunion, afraid that Joseph might seek revenge.

For a moment, Joseph hesitated. Should he put his brothers to the test as to their sincerity and change of heart? Joseph decided jealousy and distrust had gone on for too long, and put his brothers at ease, "Fear not, I am glad to see you. How is our father?" The brothers reported that Jacob was well, except that the whole family suffered from the devastating country-wide famine.

Joseph instructed his men to load to the hilt the bags his brothers had brought with them and added twelve donkeys fully laden for the brothers to take home. "If you run out of supplies, come back for more or, if you prefer, you are welcome to settle here in Egypt," Joseph said.

The brothers looked at each other in amazement, and Reuben spoke up, "How come you are so kind to us, when we almost killed you and sold you into slavery?"

Joseph replied, "Even though you have been mean to me, I had a part in it, since I enjoyed being in the role of father's favorite son. In my heart I forgave you long ago, even as I hope you forgave me. Everything is working out for the best in my life. I am happily married, the father of two sons, and Pharaoh appointed me governor of Egypt. Perhaps you were the instruments of my destiny. Trouble yourselves no more and let us celebrate our happy reunion." And they sat down for a banquet of peace and thanksgiving, renewing the family ties in a spirit of mutual forgiveness.

CHAPTER THREE
FROM SLAVERY TO FREEDOM

Prologue: Liberty For All

The exodus of the Israelites from Egyptian bondage is a momentous event that has formed the consciousness of the Jews for thousands of years. It is a symbol also of other freedom odysseys, particularly the civil rights movement. Martin Luther King has been called the Moses of Black America.

Looking back upon the dramatic escape of the Israelites from Egyptian bondage, the odds seemed so great against it, that in popular imagination, only the guiding, protecting hand of God could achieve such a feat. When all human efforts fail, that which appears impossible becomes possible with God. Hence, the Israelites fantasized about a series of spectacular, supernatural interventions like plagues upon Pharaoh and the destruction of the pursuing Egyptians in the Sea of Reeds. While the waters opened up for the fleeing Israelites, they closed in on Egyptian chariots and horsemen. Legend has stressed divine miracles, rather than the Israelites taking credit for practical qualities like their singleness of purpose, resourcefulness and discipline. To claim those virtues would have sounded like bragging or being ungrateful to God.

Liberation, to be sure, is a glorious experience. However, trouble looms when in the struggle for freedom, the oppressed turn into executioners, oppressors into victims. The Old Testament records that God first hardened the heart of Pharaoh and then, in retaliation for his stubbornness, Egypt was visited by a series of outrageous, God-sent plagues. The delight with which the punishment of Egypt was greeted by the Israelites undermined the triumphant achievement of the exodus. The god of Moses did not merely inflict heavy retribution upon Egypt, Jehovah became a war god for the conquest of the promised land. The Egyptians and Canaanites became victims of the exodus.

The lesson in this segment of the Bible is that one nation's gain is another country's loss. Such a perspective is primitive, as opposed to the higher concept where every nation is God's concern.

1.
No Need To Explain: "I Am Who I Am"

The famine in Canaan brought thousands of Israelites to Egypt and many of them, like Joseph, prospered in the new homeland.

The Israelites were grateful to Egypt for the opportunity to escape the affliction visited upon Canaan and did their best to serve the host country. Yet, as the Israelites were fruitful and multiplied, their increased numbers and skills made some Egyptians afraid and envious. Eventually, the pharaohs turned against the Israelites, enlisting them for the building of pyramids, thinking that harsh slave labor would break their backbone. The Israelites, however, withstood the rigors and continued to grow in number and strength.

Frustrated, Ramses II decided to resort to a policy of genocide. A decree went forth that all newborn male Israelites should be drowned. This sent terror into the hearts of the Israelites. Countless babes were killed.

One couple from the house of Levi hid a son for three months and, finally, in despair, rather than drown the baby, placed the child in an ark of bulrushes and floated it down the river, hoping that someone might take pity on it.

As the daughter of the Pharaoh came to wash herself at the stream, she saw the ark, sent her maid to fetch it and, behold, the babe wept. She was compassionate, raised him as her son, and called his name

Moses, which in Egyptian means "son" and in Hebrew "because I drew him out of the water."

Moses, born of Levites and raised like a prince in the household of Pharaoh's daughter, was confused. Who was the real me? What was the decisive influence, the bonds of blood or of upbringing? One day, Moses went out to the working place, and saw an Egyptian overseer abuse a Hebrew slave. Abruptly, all hesitations ceased. He resolved to side with his victimized people and help them some day to gain their freedom. Meanwhile, he needed to put distance between himself and the imperial court. Moses fled to dwell in the land of Midian in the southern tip of the Sinai Peninsula.

Moses settled there, got married, and one day, leading the flock of his father-in-law, came to Horeb, a craggy, imposing mountain range. There he had the uncanny vision of a burning bush, aflame with fire, yet not consumed. Moses was startled and wondered whether it was symbolic of the burning slavery of his people, an oppression that kept on and on, while Moses was enjoying a quiet family life, tending flocks at a safe distance from Egypt.

Out of the burning bush, God challenged Moses:

"I am the God of Abraham and Sarah, Isaac, Rebecca, Jacob and Rachel. I have seen the affliction of my people under the taskmasters. I want them delivered from the yoke of bondage, and have chosen you, Moses, to plead the cause of the Israelites before Pharaoh and lead them back into the land of your forebears."

Moses was unconvinced, "Who am I that I should go unto the Pharaoh and bring forth the children of Israel out of Egypt?" God responded, "Fear not, the divine spirit of humanity that abhors oppression and loves freedom will be upon you."

Moses' resistance started to wane. The scene of his Hebrew brothers beaten by a brutal taskmaster flashed back. Moses had one last question. How would the Israelites believe him, that he had been appointed to lead them out of slavery? "When they ask 'who sent you,' what shall I reply?"

God answered, "You do not need to explain, just say 'I am who I am.'"

2.
On Behalf of the Oppressed: "Let My People Go"

Emboldened by his visions, Moses left for Egypt to plead before Pharaoh, "Let my people go."

It was not only that Pharaoh's heart was hardened, there were economic factors involved. He wanted to complete work on the pyramids and other building projects and instructed the overseers to make the slaves work even harder.

Moses was upset that his appeal merely worsened the conditions of the Israelites. It came to pass that a volcanic eruption occurred in the upper Nile region, thrusting lava and red earth into the river, making it look like blood. The fish died, creating panic in the population and concern among the Egyptian authorities. Moses seized the occasion to return to Pharaoh, saying, "See, the pollution of the Nile is a divine sign to let my people go." Yet, the emperor's heart remained stubborn. The volcanic action also resulted in the river's overflowing, eventually causing a plague of mosquitoes that attacked people and animals. Moses saw this as another opportunity to present his case, but once more to no avail.

Additional calamities succeeded each other; plagues of frogs, gadflies and locusts, death striking Egyptian livestock, crops destroyed by hailstorms, boils covering the skin of the people, clouds of ashes darkening the skies.

Each time Moses returned with the request, "Let my people go," yet nothing seemed to change pharaoh's determination.

The worst was yet to come. Weakened by the diverse plagues visited upon the land, children started to die on a massive scale. This sent shockwaves of ter-

ror through the land, for without youth the very survival of Egypt was at stake.

The spectacle of innocent children dying was too much for Moses. He did not have the heart to suggest that God might inflict such extreme hardships even for the worst of crimes. Moses remembered how he, as an infant, had been saved by Pharaoh's daughter. He recalled Israelites preserved from famine by Egypt's hospitality. None of the plagues had moved Pharaoh's hardened heart. So Moses decided to change his approach.

Instead of continuing to seek permission from the authorities, he would start on the assumption the Israelites were entitled to freedom, and to return to the land they had left because of famine. Rather than beg for what belonged to them rightfully, the Israelites would take destiny into their hands and organize themselves for the exodus.

Moses met in secret council with other leaders of his people. Together they agreed upon a time when all the Israelites would gather along with their herds to leave the land of present affliction. The date was set for the anniversary of the Israelite migration to Egypt. The sons and daughters of Israel would gather by the thousands so that the Egyptians would be hard put to prevent the flight. There was also the element of surprise. By the time the Egyptians would be able to react, the Israelites could be out of immediate danger. What neither eloquence, threats nor plagues could achieve was brought about by clear thinking, efficient planning, human dedication and national unity. And the Israelites departed peacefully from Egypt to return to the promised land.

3.
Path to Freedom: Wandering in the Wilderness

Tradition has it that the Israelites wandered in the wilderness for forty years. Often the people endured hunger and thirst. Repeatedly they grumbled against

Moses for leading them away from the relative security, abundance and civilization of Egypt to the uncertainties and primitive conditions of the wilderness.

Early in their wanderings, the Israelites were pursued by Egyptian horsemen and had a narrow escape crossing swampy waters and treacherous sand dunes that were to become a grave to Egyptian chariots. This almost miraculous deliverance impressed itself deeply upon the consciousness of the Israelites.

Somehow, whatever the dangers and hardships of the historic march from bondage to freedom, it seemed as if God's protecting hand was stretched out over the people, and as though Moses' resourcefulness was equal to every occasion.

The greatest test came at Mount Sinai when Moses, on a beautiful, balmy day, climbed up to the resplendent, sunny summit to experience revelation from on high and out of the depths of his own being.

As in his vision of the burning bush, Moses had another human-divine encounter, and the message he received was in the form of the Ten Commandments:

> Thou shalt have no other gods before me
> Thou shalt not make a graven image
> Thou shalt not take the name of God in vain
> Thou shalt keep the sabbath
> Thou shalt honor thy parents
> Thou shalt not murder
> Thou shalt not commit adultery
> Thou shalt not steal
> Thou shalt not commit perjury
> Thou shalt not covet

These commandments seemed so vital to Moses that he wrote them down on tablets of stone to give his people an eternal reminder of what it takes to bring individuals and nations in harmony with the divine.

4.
Temptation: The Golden Calf

The Ten Commandments were the outcome of forty days spent by Moses on the mountaintop, listening to the voices of his conscience and God. Meanwhile, the Israelites encamped at the foot of the mountain became restless. When the people saw that their leader delayed coming down, they said to Moses' brother, Aaron, "We feel abandoned and want visible gods fashioned out of precious metals to go before us for protection."

Aaron was taken off balance by this rebellious upsurge, and hoping to calm the crowd, said, "Break off your golden earrings and with them I shall make a graven image; a golden calf that will lead us out of the wilderness." The people of Israel danced around the molten animal Aaron had fashioned, and worshipped it as their idol.

Upon descending from the lofty heights of Mount Sinai, Moses found his followers engaged in the sinful worship of a graven image. Moses was furious. He had led the Israelites safely out of bondage in Egypt and had enabled them to survive against severe odds. Now, upon the first occasion when Moses had left on a brief, important mission to commune with God and conscience, the people gave up their faith in the living God of creation and freedom to worship a substitute god of gold.

In his anger, Moses smashed the stone tablets of the Ten Commandments and destroyed the golden calf.

5.
Moses: "I Have Been To The Mountain Top"

As Moses' anger simmered down, he decided to go back to the mountain top and reflect on the situation. Moses reasoned that even though the Israelites had become worshippers for a moment of an idol, such backsliding did not abolish God's promise to lead them out of bondage to the land of freedom.

Moses wondered also on how to make the Ten Commandments more positive. Orders of "thou shalt" and prohibitions like "thou shalt not," along with an aura of authority, could elicit a temptation to rebel. From the beginning, the approach had not worked, as when Adam and Eve were forbidden to eat the apple from the tree of knowledge. So Moses decided to express his ideas in a caring way:

> Love your neighbor as yourself.
> Love life with all your mind, heart and strength.
> Remember the seventh day of creation and keep it holy.
> Honor your father and mother and be good to your siblings.
> Do unto others as you would have others do unto you.
> Be affectionate and faithful toward the person you love.
> Be a steward of this earth and its richness.
> Live in peace and without violence.
> Speak truth in kindness.
> All human beings are entitled to equal rights and dignity.

Once again Moses returned from the mountain top to be with his people. Yet, instead of engraving the guidelines for happiness in tablets of stone, he wrote them into the hearts of the Israelites. As Moses descended from the heights of Mount Sinai, his face shone radiantly, expressing forgiveness for past shortcomings and the promise of a bright and better future.

CHAPTER FOUR
PEACE IS THE WAY

Prologue: Modeling War or Peace

Myth is a way of describing reality, not to be confused with its nature or essence. There are different ways of perceiving the world, hence different mythologies. If a culture or an individual sees reality differently from Biblical authors, it makes sense to change the stories, as I have done, rewriting myths such as Adam and Eve, Cain and Abel, and Jacob and Esau.

When it comes to historical events, they cannot be altered at will. Therefore, I am retaining in basic outline the war-like conquest of Canaan under Joshua. However, when dealing with legendary figures like Samson and Delilah, Gideon, Goliath and Judith, where history mingles with mythology, it is legitimate to give free reign to creative imagination. Biblical myths and my own are similar inasmuch as they are both inventions of the human spirit. The difference lies in the fact that the Bible has in its favor the aura of authority and tradition. The advantage of a new mythology is that it inclines humankind toward a civilized future, rather than keeping us beholden to the barbarisms of the past. We need to cease being programmed for a monotonous repetition of the mistakes of our forebears.

Clearly, war is a luxury we cannot afford. Myths that exalt the glories of a war god and condone genocide in the name of religion, need to be supplanted by stories that model peaceful problem-solving.

1.
Joshua's Unholy War

God had given the Israelites a mission of peace, freedom and wisdom in a violent world of bondage and superstition. The task of the Jews was to overcome war, oppression and ignorance to show humankind how it is done.

The story of the Exodus symbolizes the yearnings of all people for liberation.

The revelation of Mount Sinai expresses the human search for enlightenment.

Moses had successfully led his people toward the promised land of liberty and wisdom.

Entrance into Canaan was the supreme test as to whether the Israelites would be able to show how to use the skills of non-violence. Alas, Joshua, Moses' successor, had an old-fashioned idea of peace, establishing it through the force of arms, conquering enemy strongholds, exterminating the other side.

Joshua's rationale looked like common sense. God had promised the land of Canaan to Abraham, Sarah and their descendants. Moses had led the Israelites out of bondage to the threshold of the new homeland. Did the Canaanites not stand in the way of divine destiny? In the name of God, they needed to be destroyed to make room for the Israelites.

Jericho was the first fortified town to be captured. It was well defended by strong walls. Joshua's troops surrounded Jericho and marched around it carrying the ark of the covenant. For seven days, seven trumpets of a ram's horn sounded. Finally, upon a signal from Joshua, the Israelite soldiers, with great shouts, burst into Jericho, massacring men and women, young and old, even the oxen, sheep and donkeys. It was the idea of a holy war in fulfillment of God's will.

Or was it? Some Israelites wondered whether Joshua's actions were not a misreading of God's intentions. "Is war ever holy?" they asked. "Is armed conflict not a way of saying that we have failed in finding peaceful means of settling disputes? Will Joshua's conquests not destroy the glory of the exodus?"

Collective violence with its victors and vanquished leads to slavery and oppression. What happens to "love thy neighbor as thyself"? It too becomes a casualty of battle. War opens up the flood gates of the lust to destroy. The taking of human lives, an act forbidden in peace, is exalted as a patriotic duty in times of hostilities. To sanctify war is to unleash the forces of death and destruction and doing it with a good conscience.

After the fall of strategically important Jericho, Joshua pushed on to take full advantage of this gain and allow his people to settle in the promised land. Bethel, Ai, Gibeon and its confederate towns were conquered in due course. Alarmed by the advance of the Israelites, a coalition of towns was formed to oppose the invaders, but the defenders were routed. The battle was so decisively to the advantage of the Israelites, that legend has it Joshua invoked God to make the sun stand still to give the Israelites daylight to complete the slaughter of the vanquished Canaanites.

Joshua sincerely believed that all this fighting was a sacred duty. The holy spirit, liberator from slavery and source of wisdom had become a god of war, destroyer, conqueror. Sometimes, as in Jericho, Joshua interpreted divine will as the total extermination of the natives. At other times, as with the Gibeonites, they were made into vassals.

At first the Canaanites remained in possession of some fortified towns, including Jerusalem. Also the god of the Canaanites, Baal, exercised a strong attraction upon many Israelites. The Hebrew god seemed supreme as a god of history, the desert and the wandering tribes. When it came to changing from a nomadic existence to settling on the land, Baal as a god of fertility appeared to have the edge. Indeed, the Israelites learned from the Canaanites how to till the

45

soil. For a long time the temptation of combining their own god and Baal or switching to Baal altogether was strong. To counteract this, there was a constant emphasis that the God of the Israelites was the only one, a jealous God. Hence, the intolerance of the ancient Israelites as a way of defending themselves against what they considered corruption, the worship of foreign gods and idols. Likewise, with Joshua's policy of either extermination of the Canaanites or their total submission. Temporarily, Joshua prevailed. The meaning of the exodus, that no one has the right to lord it over fellow human beings, was lost for the time being. The message of Mount Sinai, love, peace and gentleness, was pushed back for now. In the long run, on the seventh day of creation, the God of peace will prevail.

2.
Gideon: Deliverer From The Scourge of War

When Joshua died at the ripe old age of one hundred and ten, the conquest of Canaan had not been completed. The Canaanites were still in possession of many fortified towns and used superior armor, such as chariots, against which the Israelites were at a disadvantage. Gradually, the Canaanites were even pushing back the Israelites. It took a major effort under the leadership of Judge Deborah to complete the Hebrew conquest of Canaan. The campaign was recorded in Deborah's victory song, depicting the slaying of the last of Canaanite kings, with his mighty army either destroyed in battle or drowned in the river Kishon.

The Israelites were now ready to settle permanently on the land. They expected to give themselves to peaceful pursuits and enjoy the fruits of their labor. However, the increasing prosperity and abundant harvests provoked the greed of neighboring tribes. Swarms of Midianites and Amalekites descended upon the land like locusts, carrying off cattle, plundering and driving the Israelites to the hills and caves in search of *shelter.* It was an ironic reversal of events. First the Israelites under Joshua, emerging from the desert, were warlike and on the attack against the Canaanites. Now, as settlers bent on peaceful pursuits, they were being driven from the land by marauding nomads.

In time of need, Israelites had often rallied around inspired leaders, persuaded to become instruments of God's will, first Abraham and Moses, then Joshua and Deborah, and now Gideon, the Deliverer. Like Moses, Gideon needed some persuading to leave his ordinary occupation as a farmer. It was as if a messenger of God spoke to him, "Save Israel out of the hand of Midian." A man of courage, the son of clan chief, Joash, Gideon still hesitated before the enormity of the task of repelling the devastating expeditions of the Midianites.

And it came to pass that Gideon took a first step by building an altar and calling it "God is peace." In the tradition of Joshua and Deborah, Israel was led by a god of war, who performed mighty, miraculous and victorious deeds on the battlefield. However, Gideon remembered God's covenant of peace with Abraham. Gideon's mission was to defend home and harvest against the attacks of the Midianites, and do it by peaceful means.

Gideon's initial impulse was to raise a large army of ablebodied men. Some thirty thousand people would be his goal. Yet, if the words "God is peace" meant anything, it was searching for a better solution than a military contest. So, instead of a general mobilization, Gideon issued a call for three hundred women and men known for their character, wisdom, eloquence and compassion to meet with Midianite leaders and negotiate a settlement.

The camp of the Midianites was in the valley of Shechem. During the night, under cover of darkness, Gideon and his company of three hundred descended from the highlands, armed only with trumpets and pitchers in which each person carried a concealed torch. Gideon's group surrounded the camp from all sides.

Gideon instructed his people, "When I sound the horn, you do likewise, when I light and brandish my torch, so will you. Then let us all shout mightily: 'Shalom—Peace'."

The penetrating sound of the trumpets awoke the Midianites who found themselves surrounded by the threatening sight of torches. The Midianites feared they had been delivered into the hands of a superior force of Israelites. Should the Midianites wage uncertain battle in the night, or abandon camp and flee to fight another day? Above the din of the trumpets, and beside the ominous torchlight, they could hear the shouts of shalom. Amid the confusion, some of the Midianite leaders called for calm and, echoing the cry "peace," came out of their tents to meet with Gideon's men and women.

Gideon and his group of counselors impressed upon the Midianites that the Israelites were unwilling to put up with further harassment. Under Gideon's leadership, they were determined to repel any further aggression and pursue the attackers. Yet, if the Midianites were willing, there could be peace and goodwill between them and the Israelites. And so it was. Rather than a bloodbath and continued enmity, reason prevailed and the Midianites became good neighbors. Gideon was called the deliverer, not only from the attacks of the Midianites, but also from the scourge of war. Gideon returned to the altar "God is peace." He gave thanks for the blessings of a peaceful outcome, in which no blood had been shed, and the former enemies had been made into friendly partners.

The Israelites were so overjoyed that they came to Gideon saying, "Rule over us, you and your sons and daughters." Gideon replied, "It is not I who shall reign, nor my sons and daughters; let peace be your ruler and guide."

And so it came to pass that under the inspired leadership of Gideon, the covenant of God with Abraham to show the world the ways of peace was *fulfilled. The Israelites and their neighbors lived for the time being as if it were the seventh day of creation.*

3.
Love Conquers All: Samson and Delilah

When the Israelites came out of Egypt and settled in the promised land, they encountered native Canaanites. Other tribes like the Moabites, Midianites and Philistines also were competing for the land.

The Israelites debated among themselves, "How shall we deal with this situation? We have wandered in the desert for four decades. There is a need to develop roots. Do we displace the present inhabitants, struggle in war for the possession of the land, or do we live side by side with the natives and other tribes that wish to settle here? Even if we accept them, will they welcome us?"

There was no simple, easy solution. In the coastal regions, the land was contested by the Philistines. Many Israelites thought of them as a threat, an enemy, a warlike tribe, eager to do battle and use any means necessary to make the Israelites into vassals.

Others, and Samson was among them, counseled conciliation. Samson's voice was important, for he was known for great strength, character and lack of fear.

Samson wished to test his hopes of working out a peaceful solution. He mingled with some Philistines, establishing contacts and making friends with them. On one such occasion, Samson met Delilah, a young, intelligent Philistine woman, whose heart was equally bent on peace and friendship. They became emotionally close, shared ideals, fell in love with each other and began to talk about getting married.

The parents of both Samson and Delilah were greatly alarmed and tried to dissuade the lovers. When ordinary persuasion failed, some Philistine chiefs decided upon a ruse. They offered Delilah beautiful gifts if only she would consent to see Samson no more.

Many Philistine chiefs feared Samson as being of a

race standing in the way of their possession of the land. Hence, there should be no mingling with the Israelites. The Israelites, as God's chosen people, frowned upon mixing with tribes that indulged in idol worship.

Delilah loved Samson dearly and so she refused the gifts and told Samson about the plot. Samson was angry and, for a moment, considered using his great strength to kill his opponents. That would teach them a lesson not to use devious methods. Yet, by spreading havoc in the ranks of the Philistines, many friends and relatives of his beloved Delilah would also be harmed. Samson remembered that it used to be thought "an eye for an eye and a tooth for a tooth," but all this accomplished was a vicious circle, creating misery over and over again. Hatred breeds more enmity, vengeance is followed by revenge. "Where there is no vision of peace, the people perish," Samson thought. So he opened his heart to Delilah that together they might come up with other ways. "Let us not settle this conflict by involving thousands of people in suffering and warfare." After much reflection, Samson and Delilah decided that Delilah would ask the Philistines to appoint the strongest man they could muster to wrestle with Samson according to some mutually acceptable rules. If Samson prevailed, the Philistines would bless the marriage; if not, it would be a sign that Samson and Delilah stop seeing one another. The proposal was clearly preferable to the impending doom of wholesale destruction.

The date of the contest was set for ninety days hence, and the two adversaries trained mightily for the match. Tales of Samson's awesome strength had spread anguish in the ranks of the Philistines, and they wondered whether he was so strong on account of some secret, magic power. As the Philistines observed Samson, they noticed one distinguishing feature, an extraordinary length of hair, that gave him an aura of authority and invincibility. The Philistines began to figure that if they could clip Samson's hair, he would have a less imposing presence.

A delegation of Philistines went to Delilah pleading, "Samson, with that lion's mane, has an unfair advantage. When Samson sleeps in your arms, will you cut off seven strands?" Delilah was happy that the Philistines had gone along at all with the offer of a peaceful contest. Two months before the wrestling was to take place, she snipped off some of Samson's hair.

The following morning, when Samson started training, he found himself terribly weak. Delilah now realized that unwittingly she might be the cause of Samson's demise and losing her beloved friend. She felt saddened at the trick, and Samson's anger welled up. He was tempted to call off the whole plan. However, as the day of the contest drew nigh, Samson, with intensive training, became stronger again, even as his hair grew back.

Finally, the hour arrived. Both sides flocked in great numbers to watch the contest. There were parades, cheerleaders, music, and even a banquet was prepared to celebrate whatever the outcome would be.

The struggle was a see-saw battle. In the end, the jury declared Samson the winner.

In one sense, the Philistines were depressed, but there was also a feeling of pride that their Delilah would be married to such a valiant man.

So the Philistines joined in the applause and sat down at the table to celebrate the peaceful settlement of the conflict.

Samson and Delilah were happily married and for many years the Philistines and the Israelites lived harmoniously side by side in the land of Canaan, where the will of God and the skill of the inhabitants made milk and honey flow.

4.
Reconciliation: David and Goliath

During the reign of King Saul, there was many a battle between the Israelites and the Philistines. For a while, the affection between Samson and Delilah led to a truce and helped overcome the enmity. Yet, many Philistines were restless. It came to pass that in the ranks of their army, a giant more than nine feet tall, Goliath of Gath, had made a name for himself as an invincible foe.

One day he stood in resplendent armor at the top of a hill, shouting unto the armies of Israel gathered on the other side of the valley of Elah: "Choose a person to engage in combat with me. If your man prevails, our armies will withdraw fifty miles and the territory is yours. If I win, your soldiers will retreat peacefully by the same distance and the land will belong to us."

King Saul and the Israelites were dismayed, for since the days of Samson they had no match for Goliath. Goliath issued the challenge daily and the morale of the Israelites sank lower and lower.

One morning David, a shepherd of the root of Jesse, delivering some supplies to Saul's troops, overheard Goliath once more vaunting his strength and challenging anyone to engage him in battle. David was only an adolescent and, compared to the massive build of Goliath, of frail stature. However, as a shepherd, he had had to contend with predators and, thanks to his resourcefulness, had slain animals of prey. Seeing that no one else was willing to take on Goliath, David let it be known that he was ready.

King Saul, impressed with David's self-confident demeanor, accepted the offer and equipped him with the king's bronze helmet, breastplate and sword. Alas, being a shepherd rather than a seasoned soldier, David was weighted down by the heavy armor and had to take it off.

Instead, David chose a staff, picked five smooth stones from the river bed, put them in his purse and, with his sling, went to meet his adversary. Goliath, in turn, walked toward David and could not believe his eyes. He had expected a robust enemy and, instead, saw a mere youth, a boy of fresh complexion and pleasant bearing. Goliath was full of scorn and felt insulted: "Am I a dog for you to come against me with sticks?"

David, unperturbed, took out a stone, slung it and swept Goliath's sword out of his right hand. With another well-aimed shot at his shinbone, he caused the giant to crash to the ground, in great pain. David rushed toward his opponent, seized the sword, saying, "I could kill you, yet I worship a God of mercy who made a covenant with my people; we could settle in this land, provided we were peaceful in our dealings with other tribes, nations, religions. We are not to shed blood, nor perpetuate enmity and vengeance. Rather than the clash of swords, I offer you the handshake of reconciliation."

Goliath, at first, felt humiliated. This little Israelite shepherd had brought him to his knees. He was angry to have been outwitted. Yet, along with the feelings of shame, there came upon him a sense of awe over the generous offer of peace, gratitude that, even in defeat, his life would be spared. Despite his pain, the giant of Gath drew himself up to full stature, took off his armor and for all the soldiers of both armies to see, David and Goliath shook hands like friends.

5.
Judith: Heroine for Peace

Nebuchadnezzar of Assyria was one of the great conquerors of history, an absolute monarch, quick to anger if anyone dared resist his sovereign will.

Holofernes was the general-in-chief of the armies and Nebuchadnezzar instructed him, "Take about one hundred and twenty thousand foot soldiers and twelve thousand cavalrymen. The feet of my soldiers and horses will cover the whole face of the earth, and I will plunder it. Rivers, blocked with dead enemies, will overflow."

Holofernes did as told, butchering all who offered resistance, burning habitations, destroying places of worship, setting fire to the harvest, killing flocks and herds, sacking towns, raping women and putting prisoners to the sword. It was a policy of the scorched earth and total, merciless war.

When Judah heard how Nebuchadnezzar's army had treated various nations, the Israelites set up defensive positions and prayed to God for help. Holofernes, learning that the Israelites had fortified the high peaks, feared that the Assyrian army might incur severe casualties, if it proceeded by frontal attack. Hence, he decided upon cutting off the water supply of the defenders. Deprived of water, the Israelites would be forced to surrender sooner or later.

After a siege for thirty-four days of Judah's forward position in Bethulia, the beleaguered Israelites were prostrate with thirst and ready to give up, when a woman, highly respected in the community, a widow named Judith, stepped forward. She perceived the situation as one where God was testing the faith of the Israelites, hence, her first move was to pray:

> "See the Assyrians boasting in their army, glorifying in horses and riders, exulting in the strength of their infantry. Trust as they may in shield and spear, in bow and sling, in You they have not recognized the God of peace and justice. Your strength does not lie in numbers, nor might in violent men. You are the God of the humble, the help of the oppressed, the support of the weak, the refuge of the forsaken, the savior of those close to despair. So, please, God of our forebears, hear my prayer, give me the strength and intelligence to prevail against these cruel opponents."

As Judith was deeply steeped in prayer, she began to see a way out of the desperate situation. She would wander into the camp of the Assyrians, speak to Holofernes and seek to win him over. Judith set out to the Assyrian side, was apprehended by an enemy patrol and asked to see Holofernes to bring him an important message. The Assyrian soldiers were not sure *whether to comply. Yet, impressed by Judith's sincere plea, they took her before their chief.*

Judith had imagined that Holofernes would behave like a blood-thirsty tyrant and was surprised to find him polite, acting like an ordinary human being. Holofernes, in turn, was taken by Judith's beauty. Her initial thought was to invite Holofernes to seduce her and behead him when his defenses were down. The Assyrians, deprived of their commander, would be in a state of shock and might flee in disarray, lifting the siege of the land. As Judith was going over this in her mind, she remembered the covenant of Abraham with God, that in exchange for the promised land, the Israelites would be a peaceful nation and abjure violence.

"Holofernes," she said, "I know you have been asked by your king to conquer Assyria's neighbors. You don't need to prove yourself anymore. You already have laid waste all who have opposed you. Why not quit while you are ahead? We, the Israelites, are a stubborn nation that has survived many a conqueror. You may win a temporary victory, but we will rise again and drive you out of our homeland. Why go through an endless cycle of suffering, when right now we can save thousands of Assyrian and Israelite lives? If you are willing to lift the siege, we will let you go without pursuing you or harming you."

Holofernes was impressed with Judith's compelling logic. It was time to end the warfare. The next morning Holofernes gave orders to dismantle the camps and head homeward. Judith rejoined her people at Bethulia, who celebrated their unexpected deliverance from starvation and death. All of Judah rejoiced, and the High Priest and the Council of Elders in Jerusalem traveled to Bethulia to give thanks to Judith and blessed her, saying:

"You are the joy of Jerusalem,
 the highest honor of our race."

Judith responded with a song of thanksgiving:

> *"Praise God with the tambourine,*
> *sing to God with the cymbal,*
> *let psalm and canticle mingle.*
> *God is a God of peace who shatters war.*
> *God is a God of joy who overcomes suffering.*
> *I will sing a new song to my God*
> *who is mercy and loving kindness."*

Judith was greatly admired for her valor on behalf of peace and died, decades later, at a ripe old age. When she passed on, the people of Israel mourned for seven days. She lives in the memory of all.

CHAPTER FIVE
THE GLORY AND PITY OF RULERS

Prologue: The Price of Power and Powerlessness

Knowledge is power, yet in the Biblical narrative of old, there is the initial paradox that eating from the tree of knowledge brings about humanity's downfall. Is it God's will to keep people in ignorance? Does divinity aspire to a monopoly of dominion and wisdom?

Strangely enough, God's rule is ambiguous. It enabled the glorious exodus from slavery. Yet, according to the Scriptures, it was also responsible for the tragic destruction of Jerusalem and the Babylonian captivity. How far are we willing to go with Biblical prophets who claim that the sufferings of the Jews are God's punishment for their sins? Taken to its ultimate conclusion, the horrors of the Holocaust would be expressions of divine omnipotence and justice. What a demonic thought that the Nazi gas chambers were instruments of God.

While power tends to corrupt, the lack of it can be equally damaging. Even as strength may lead to abuse, weakness invites persecution. Hebrew bondage in Egypt is a symbol of powerlessness. When the Israelites leave for freedom in the promised land, they displace and destroy the Canaanites. There need to be other choices than the traditional one of being hammer or anvil, executioner or victim.

The period of supreme Israelite power in ancient history was during the reigns of the first three kings, yet those decades are marked by tragedy. Saul had a streak of insanity and ended up committing suicide on the battlefield. David had to flee his own son, Absalom, as well as King Saul, and embarked upon the conquest of neighboring countries. Solomon's wealth exceeded his proverbial wisdom. The luxury of his lifestyle led to forced labor, when the purpose of the exodus had been escape from slavery.

Monarchs were symbols of power and national unity, flashes of brilliance that lit up the firmament of history, yet ended like meteors that self-destruct. Power needs to serve, while the temptation of royal rule is to exploit. Saul's melancholy madness, David's lust for conquest, Solomon's love of accumulating and displaying wealth made the chosen people no different from other nations. Perhaps the lesson is that all people are elected; every nation is called to be peaceful. When the whole burden is placed on Israel alone or its kings, they collapse under the weight. Such is the glory and pity of Saul, Solomon and David.

Royalty started with a desire to bring together the twelve tribes of Israel, something the era of the judges had not been able to achieve. For a while, the kings established a central government; a common defense; a capital city, Jerusalem; and a place of worship for the whole nation—Solomon's Temple.

The new-found unity under the leadership of strong monarchs did not endure. Israel split asunder, northern and southern kingdoms became rivals. The ten tribes founded their own sanctuaries, Bethel and Dan. Shechem was made into a political capital, in opposition to the city of David. At one point, Judah even joined militarily with the Syrians against the northern kingdom.

Solomon was the last king of a united Israel. With division came weakness. Both fragments were overpowered by aggressive empires. The northern kingdom fell under the rod of Assyria in 722, Before the Common Era (B.C.E.). About a century and a half later, Judah of the Davidic line came to an end with the destruction of Jerusalem and the Babylonian captivity.

1.
From Samuel the Priest to Saul the King

The fertile crescent of the promised land had been an attraction to many tribes, empires, nations, among them the Philistines who eventually gave the land the name of Palestine. The Philistines were sea people, inhabitants of the coast of Asia Minor and Aegean Islands. Displaced by the westward migration of Aryan people, repelled when attempting to make a homeland for themselves in Egypt, the Philistines settled along the coastal plains of the land of Canaan. Gradually they pushed forward into the highlands where the Israelites lived.

Despite some goodwill on both sides, as evidenced by the happy union of Samson and Delilah, the pressures of conflicting territorial ambitions asserted themselves. In the contest, the Israelites proved no match for the superior military strength of the Philistines. This came as a bitter surprise to the Israelites, since they had been able to prevail against the Canaanites and thought that God would help them overcome any odds. One explanation for the failure of the Hebrews to stand on their own was the self-accusation that they must have sinned, and not lived up to the demands of God and had made concessions to the Canaanite god, Baal. The Philistine advance and conquest was seen as a punishment for Israel's shortcomings.

Several generations had come and gone since Gideon, the deliverer from the Midianites. Who would rally the Israelites and protect them from the yoke of the Philistines?

In those days, in the hill country of Ephraim, there lived a woman named Hannah and her husband, Elkanah. To Hannah's great grief, she was childless, but vowed that if she ever had a son, he would be dedicated to the service of God. And it came to pass that Hannah bore a son. She named the child Samuel and had him groomed to be God's servant. Indeed, as Samuel grew up, he became a seer, prophet, judge and priest.

Samuel, the seer, had the gift of foretelling the future. In his capacity as judge, he united the Israelites in defense against the Philistines. As a prophet, he was believed to speak for God. Samuel, the priest, anointed Saul to be the first king of the Israelites.

Early in life, Samuel's family had settled at Shiloh, an important religious center situated some twenty-five miles to the north of Jerusalem. Samuel was about twenty years old, when the Philistines razed Shiloh to the ground and carried off one of the holiest Israelite objects of worship—the ark of the covenant. It was as if the glory had departed from Israel. The government by a succession of judges from Joshua to Samuel was no longer working. The clans and tribes were too isolated to survive. It was out of this need for unity that Samuel anointed Saul.

Just as Moses was God's choice to lead the Israelites out of bondage in Egypt, Saul was to become king as a God-appointed deliverer from the oppression of the Philistines. Samuel announced and fulfilled the transition from the rule of judges to the reign of kings.

Deep down, Samuel was ambivalent about what he was doing. Along with the advantage of having a king, Samuel perceived potential dangers. Samuel feared that to establish a kingdom was a way of becoming "like other nations." It was customary for monarchs to vie for prestige and place a heavy financial burden upon the people. There was the danger that a king, rather than God, would become the supreme ruler of Israel.

Initially, Saul was able to prevail against the Philistines and contain the neighbors, the Moabites, Amalekites, Edomites, bringing respite to the hard-pressed children of Israel. Samuel's anointing of Saul was singularly propitious. Yet, even in victory, Samuel became concerned. King Saul, once established in *power, used his own judgment, rather than follow the ideas of Samuel and the priesthood.*

An old tradition, accepted by Joshua in Jericho, was to put the enemy under the ban. This meant that it was the religious duty of the Israelites to kill not only opposing soldiers, but civilians as well; women and children. From this perspective, booty was to be utterly destroyed, not used for the benefit of the victors, not even for a sacrifice to God.

Samuel went along with this concept, while Saul was more generous in victory. Saul spared the life of Agag, king of Amalek and his own son, Jonathan, at the risk of violating an oath. Saul also kept the best of the herds. Such violations of ancient religious traditions made Samuel turn against Saul.

Saul was deeply hurt when Samuel, who had anointed him, withdrew approval and support. Saul had saved his people from foreign domination. He had shown himself more humane toward the vanquished than was the custom in his times. Rejection by Samuel was hard for Saul. What good was it to be accepted as a powerful king, when God, the priesthood and close friends like Samuel seemed opposed to him? Saul became depressed, desolate, brooding, jealous, distrustful, even mentally unstable; a sad state of mind for Israel's first king, who had accomplished so much for the people. The pressures of war, rigid priestly beliefs, burdens of the highest office overwhelmed Saul. He died on the battlefield of self-inflicted wounds. Alongside the glory of being king, Saul came to experience the pity of it all.

2.
David: Humble Shepherd, Mighty Conqueror

After David's successful contest with Goliath, his fame spread like wildfire throughout Israel. To kill Goliath would have been the ways of the world, victory through superior strength or smartness. David's tri-

umph was of a higher order, giving the handshake of peace, reconciling a former enemy.

King Saul was happy that David had saved face for the Israelites, yet David's popularity also rankled the king. He began to feel less appreciated than David, who had great personal charm, an ability to develop warm friendships. Jonathan, one of Saul's sons, became David's best friend. Michael, Saul's daughter, fell in love and married David. Resentful, King Saul started to plot David's death. Somehow the longstanding conflict with the Philistines and burdens of being king, were too much. Saul lost his grip on reality, and after vain hope that his rival might die on the battlefield, he asked Jonathan to kill David. Torn between obedience toward his father and deep affection for David, Jonathan chose friendship, urging David to seek safety at large. Michael did likewise, saying: "If thou savest not thy life tonight, tomorrow thou shalt be slain."

David felt hurt. He had sought to help the people; he had given loyal support to Israel's first king, only to be threatened with death. Remembering God's covenant with Abraham to settle disputes peacefully, what was David to do? He decided to flee into the wilderness, Ziph, Maon and En-gedi. By putting a distance between himself and Saul, David hoped that the king's murderous intentions would abate. Alas, Saul persisted in pursuing David and finally tracked him down.

As Saul entered David's cavernous hiding place, he was at the mercy of David's men who had him surrounded. The fugitive could now get even with his persecutor and destroy Saul. David chose to be magnanimous, for to injure Saul, David reasoned, was to harm the anointed king of Israel.

Saul graciously spared from destruction, was moved to tears, saying, "Thou art generous, David, whereas I have regarded thy good deeds with evil, thou hast rewarded my evil deeds with good."

Saul's rescue was short-lived. Soon thereafter, he

and his three sons were overwhelmed in a battle with the Philistines. Despite Saul's hostility toward him, David composed a magnificent funeral lamentation:

> "The beauty of Israel is slain;
> Saul and Jonathan were lovely and pleasant in their lives,
> And in death, they were not divided.
> How are the mighty fallen."

David now went to Hebron where he was anointed king to succeed Saul. Ishbosheth, a son of Saul, was also a pretender to the throne and ruled for several years, until murdered. David became undisputed monarch of Israel, full of promise and glory. David was a poet, musician, psalmist. He is remembered for conquering Jerusalem from the Jebusites and making it the political capital of the kingdom. Jerusalem has been called the City of David.

The king greatly extended the realm of the Israelites which under his rule, stretched from the Euphrates River in the north to the Red Sea in the south and beyond the river Jordan in the east. To prevent the loss of Jerusalem, David built up its fortifications. To enhance the importance of the city, he constructed many splendid public edifices.

David also made Jerusalem the religious capital of the nation. He brought the Ark of the Covenant to the City of Peace, providing a permanent resting place for this most sacred symbol of the Israelites.

David chose Jerusalem as the site of the Temple which, by ancient tradition, is dedicated to peace. Having taken Jerusalem by force, David was not allowed to build a permanent shrine for the Ark, a task later accomplished by David's peaceful successor, his son King Solomon.

David's rule, like Saul's was not beyond reproach. He pursued an aggressive policy of military expansion, treated women as a possession and had a streak of ruthlessness, as can be seen from the following story.

63

In those days it came to pass that David walked upon the roof of his palace and saw a beautiful woman. He inquired, "Is this not Bath-sheba, the wife of Uriah the Hittite?" David sent messengers and took her. Several weeks later, she told the king, "I am with child." David called his army commander Joab, saying, "Put Uriah in the forefront of the hottest battle and retire that he may be smitten and die." It was done. When Bath-sheba heard that her husband had been killed in battle, she mourned, then David sent after her, she became his wife and bore him a son. The offspring died within a week. Later, Bath-sheba gave birth to a second son, named Solomon.

Strange how a union that started with murder led to the birth of a king who was to be world-renowned for his wisdom.

A redeeming quality in David was repentance over his own misdeeds and at times forgiveness for those of others. When prophet Nathan pointed out the crime of causing the death of Uriah and marrying his wife, David, rather than justifying his actions, acknowledged his sins.

Another tragedy in David's life was his son's rebellion. Absalom raised an army against his father, conquered Jerusalem, sending David fleeing for his life. When the tides of battle changed and Absalom was killed, David was grief-stricken, "O, my son, Absalom! My son, my son, Absalom! Would God I had died for thee."

David, after ruling for forty years, had to face rival claims for his succession. Adonijah and Solomon, both sons of David, though of different mothers, competed in palace intrigue to win their father's favor. As Solomon became the dying monarch's choice, David on his deathbed charged his son to liquidate Joab, the distinguished commander-in-chief and Shimei, the last significant survivor of the house of Saul. Solomon obliged and added to the blood-letting his older brother, Adonijah.

Clearly, the power struggles were brutal, with little or no indication that religion softened the harshness of the conflicts. When Joshua, Saul and David had violated the divine command to show the world the ways of peace, formal honoring of God, like establishing a home in Jerusalem for the Ark of the Covenant, is an empty gesture. David failed the ultimate test of knowing how to serve peace and save the people.

Despite such shortcomings, the memory of David's illustrious qualities has been glowing for centuries. It was a time when the power of Israel was at its crest. In years of hardship, exile and foreign occupation, legend had it that some day a Messiah from the root of Jesse, the line of David would bring the nation back to its former glory.

3.
Pearls of Wisdom, Outrageous Wealth: King Solomon

At the beginning of Solomon's reign, God appeared to him in a dream, asking, "What shall I give thee?" and the king replied, "I am inexperienced. Endow thy servant with an understanding heart, that I may discern between what is of help and harm, and excel in peace."

God was pleased, answering, "King David has made vassals of foreign nations. I will bless your efforts to have good relations with them, allowing others to enjoy the freedoms you want for your own people. I used to be a jealous God. No more. You are to be accepting of religions other than that of Israel. Let everyone worship according to their highest conscience."

Encouraged by these words, Solomon felt free to build shrines where foreign wives were able to pay homage to their gods. Instead of being self-righteous, "My faith is divine, yours in error," tolerance became a way of life at Solomon's court. Such accepting attitudes helped turn Israel's destiny away from fanaticism and war.

And it came to pass that all the days of Solomon, Judah and Israel dwelt safely, every man and woman under their vine and fig tree. After centuries of strife and struggle, peace at last came to the promised land.

The change was so momentous that people would say about their new ruler, "His heart is as vast as the sand on the seashore, wise as none before him. For riches and wisdom he outshines all the kings of the earth." The queen of Sheba and the whole world sought audience of him and each would bring exquisite presents, gold and silver vessels, robes, spices and horses.

Solomon was famous for sayings and proverbs attributed to him, like "Where there is no vision, the people perish," "Who hates wisdom is in love with death," "The earnings of the wicked are fraught with anxiety," "Wisdom is more precious than pearls." A peaceful kingdom and a generous spirit in religion caused the monarch to be greatly admired.

Tolerance did not mean indifference. Solomon was devoted to his God. He prayed, worshipped, and built a resplendent dwelling place for Jehovah. The lavish decorations of the Temple were beyond anything Israel had ever seen.

Alas, in order to support his refined taste, superb Temple and luxurious court, Solomon lived beyond his means like an ostentatious despot. Just as the pharaohs needed slaves to erect extravagant pyramids, Solomon resorted to forced labor for the Temple and other impressive public buildings. Conscription and high taxation led to popular dissatisfaction. No sooner had the ruler died, than his kingdom fell apart. Such was the glory and pity of Solomon.

CHAPTER SIX
PROPHETS OF WOE AND SALVATION

Prologue: Messengers of God

Let us establish a time line as history unfolds in the promised land. From about 1250 to 1200 B.C.E., the Israelites under Joshua take possession of the land of Canaan. During the next one hundred and fifty years, the country is settled by the twelve tribes. It is the beginning of a national community under the leadership of judges like Gideon, Samson, Deborah and Samuel. Yet the tribal confederacy is loosely knit and fails to repel decisively the inroads of the Philistine and other nations. Hence the reluctant decision to create a stronger central government, headed by kings. From about 1050 to 930 B.C.E., three famous monarchs reign, Saul, David and Solomon. They represent a great increase and zenith of power. However, after initial successes, following the death of Solomon, there occurs a fateful, debilitating division between North and South, Israel and Judah. In 722 B.C.E., the northern kingdom of Israel falls to the Assyrians who carry off almost 30,000 people into captivity. In 598, Nebuchadnezzar conquers Judah including its capital Jerusalem. Eleven years later, the Holy City, rebellious despite defeat and foreign occupation, is burnt to the ground, Solomon's Temple destroyed, and the last of the kings, Zedekiah, captured, his eyes put out before being taken in chains to Babylon.

After the judges and great kings, there is a third period in the nation's destiny, prior to, during and after exile—a generation of prophets. They understood themselves to be mouthpieces of God. They were divine messengers who predicted, described and drew lessons from the hardships of Babylonian bondage. They echoed not only the sufferings of the Jews in those days, but prefigured them down to the Nazi holocaust. In broad outline, the prophets have been vindicated. Throughout history there exists a persistent pattern of persecution of the "chosen people," dispossession, expulsion, exile and genocide. After each destructive phase, there has been a period of rebuilding, even after Hitler's "final solution."

The prophetic writings constitute an important part, over one quarter of the Old Testament. In their forecast of doom and destruction, the messengers of God strike terror into our hearts. As we listen to their voices, we are tempted to react, "No, this cannot be, it is too ghastly," yet reality has gone beyond wildest oracles. Concentration camps, cattle trains and gas chambers outstripped ancient visions of devilish inhumanity.

The prophetic stance implies that the wrath of God is involved in the horror chambers of history. Retribution and vengeance are described as God's righteous response to the crimes of unfaithfulness, immorality, and social injustice. According to this view, the sins of the Israelites are writ large and account for their disastrous fate.

Blaming the Jews for their misfortunes is a troublesome perspective. Self-flagellation exceeds the bounds of welcome humility, invites inordinate guilt feelings among the victims and allows for a good conscience amid the persecutors. Jeremiah's model of submitting to chastisement as a way of obeying divine justice may at times have influenced the Jews to offer minimal resistance when led to slaughter.

The Scriptures contain the Books of four major prophets, Isaiah, Jeremiah, Ezekiel and Daniel, as well as those of twelve minor prophetic personalities. Actually, there are three distinct individuals who go under the ascribed name of Isaiah and they even lived in different centuries. Daniel, belonging more to apocalyptic literature, is included in the seventh chapter.

The encouraging part about the messengers of God is that after acknowledging the gloomy aspects of history and the grim prospects for the immediate future, the long-range outlook is one of hope and restoration, a faith doggedly kept alive to this day. Without the prophetic confidence in the final advent of a peaceful kingdom, humankind might have found it impossible to survive the dark ages of cruelty, oppression and exploitation. Alas, in the Old Testament, the prophets spend more time on punishment and destruction than on hope. A reversal in emphasis is necessary to help turn events around. With today's arsenal of chemical and nuclear doomsday machines there continues to exist a self-destructive fascination with death. What is needed is a prophetic commitment to life and peaceful problem-solving, something urgently required in the here and now.

1.
First Isaiah: The Wolf Shall Dwell With The Lamb

> *What a harlot she has become,*
> *the faithful city.*
> *Zion was all justice!*
> *Once integrity lived there,*
> *but now assassins.*
> *Your silver has turned into dross,*
> *your wine is watered.*
> *Your princes are rebels,*
> *accomplices of thieves.*
> *You may multiply your prayers.*
> *I shall not listen.*
> *Your hands are covered with blood.*
> *Take your wrongdoing out of my sight.*
> *Learn to do good,*
> *search for justice,*
> *help the oppressed,*

be just to the orphan,
plead for the widow.
Come let us reason together.
Though your sins are like scarlet,
they shall be as white as snow.
Zion will be redeemed by justice
and her penitents by integrity.
My friend had a vineyard on a hillside.
He dug the soil, cleared it of stones,
and planted choice vines in it.
In the middle he built a tower,
dug a press there too.
He expected it to yield grapes,
but sour grapes were all that it gave.
Yes, men, women and children are the vineyard of
   God.
They are that chosen plant.
God foresaw justice, but behold oppression;
wanted peace, but behold strife.
Woe to those who add house to house.
and join field to field,
until everywhere belongs to them
and they are the sole inhabitants of the land.
Woe to the legislators of infamous laws,
to those who issue tyrannical decrees,
refuse justice to the unfortunate
and cheat the poor of their rights.
Woe to those who build their hopes on cavalry,
rely on the number of chariots,
the strength of mounted men,
but never look to the Holy One.
I will put an end to the arrogance of men,
and humble the pride of despots.
Fallen, fallen is Babylon;
all the images of her gods
are shattered on the ground.
The earth is mourning,
the world pining,
the soil defiled.

*For its inhabitants have transgressed the law,
broken the everlasting covenant.
A curse consumes the earth
and its people suffer the penalty.
There is lamentation in the streets,
gladness banished from the country.
My people will go into exile:
her dignitaries dying of hunger,
her populace parched with thirst.
Yet destruction is not the last word.
The people that walked in darkness
have seen a great light.
They that dwell in the land of the shadow of death,
upon them the sun shineth.
You have increased their gladness;
they delight in your presence,
as people rejoice at harvest time.
For unto us a child is born, a son is given;
and his name shall be called
wonderful counselor, mighty God,
friend forever, prince of peace.
A shoot springs from the stock of Jesse,
on him God's spirit rests,
a spirit of wisdom and insight,
counsel and power.
He does not judge by appearances,
gives no verdict on hearsay.
The wolf shall dwell with the lamb,
the leopard lie down with the kid;
and a little child shall lead them.
They shall not hurt nor destroy
in all my holy mountain:
For the earth shall be full of divine insight,
as the waters cover the sea.
God will wipe away the tears from every cheek
and destroy death forever.*

2.
Make Straight A Highway For Peace: Second Isaiah

Comfort ye, comfort ye my people
Let the world know
That the times of struggle and warfare are over,
human sins atoned,
for the people have already received
double punishment for all their shortcomings.
A voice cries in the wilderness,
"Prepare ye the way for life,
Make straight in the desert a highway for peace.
Every valley shall be exalted,
every mountain and hill shall be made low:
the crooked straight, the rough places plain:
The glory of universal harmony shall be revealed.
All flesh is grass,
and its beauty like the wild flower's.
When the breath of death blows on them,
the grass withers, the flower fades,
but the love of life remains forever.
Lift up your voices, be not afraid,
for behold, the spirit of God is with us,
it is neither faint nor weary;
it renews the strength of those who believe in life.
Behold my servants,
in whom my soul delights.
I have endowed you with a spirit divine,
bringing peace and happiness,
I have appointed you as a covenant of the people
and light of nations,
Sing a new song,
Let its praise resound from the ends of the earth:
I will never forget you,
I will never forsake you.
How lovely are the messengers
who brings us the gospel of peace,
tidings of happiness,
good news of salvation.

I did abandon you for a brief moment,
but with great love I take you back.
In excess of anger,
I hid my face from you.
With kindness and mercy I return.
For as I have sworn
that the waters of Noah would not flood the earth again,
so I announce
that my love and concern for you shall never end,
nor shall my covenant of peace be shaken.

3.
Third Isaiah: I Create A New Heaven And Earth

Hanging your head like a reed,
lying down on sackcloth and ashes,
is that what you call fasting?
To be acceptable to God
is to break unjust fetters
and let the oppressed go free;
to share your bread with the hungry,
shelter and clothe the homeless poor,
and not turn from your own kin.
Then will your light shine like the dawn,
your wound be quickly healed,
and your shadows become like noon.
You will rebuild the ancient ruins on the old foundations.
If you refrain from trampling the sabbath,
and doing business on the holy day;
if you honor it by abstaining from travel,
from doing business and gossiping,
then shall you find happiness in God.
No, the divine hand is not too short to save,
nor the ear too dull to hear.
Like the blind we feel our way along walls,
and stumble as though noon were twilight.
Our faults in your sight have been many
and our sins are a witness against us.

We know our iniquities and our rebellion.
We have turned our back on God.
Justice is withheld
and integrity stands aloof;
in the public square sincerity is brought to its knees.
Though you have been abandoned,
hated and shunned,
I will make you a joy forever.
Violence will no longer be heard in your country,
nor devastation and ruin within your frontiers.
The spirit of God has been given to me,
God has sent me to bring good news to the poor,
bind hearts that are broken;
proclaim liberty to captives,
freedom to those in prison,
a year of divine favor.
For now I create a new Heaven and Earth,
and the miseries of the past will be forgotten.
Be glad and rejoice;
No more will the sound of weeping be heard;
I am coming to gather the nations of every
  language.

4.
Jeremiah: Death Will Seem Preferable To Life

Jeremiah is a man steeped in bitter despair. To be sure, the haunted doomsayer also predicts a silver lining, the eventual restoration and happiness of Israel. However they will come to pass only after orgies of suffering and destruction.

The divine word was addressed to Jeremiah:

"I have appointed you as a prophet to the nations." He responded: "Oh God, I do not know how to speak: I am only a youth!" And God answered: "Fear not! I will support you and put words into your mouth. Today I am setting you over kings, priests and nations to destroy and rebuild." With a heavy heart, Jeremiah accepted the call, and started to prophesy to his people:

> "You have worshiped idols of wood and stone,
> rather than the living God.
> You have as many divinities
> As you have towns, Judah,
> as many altars for Baal
> as Jerusalem has streets.
> In vain have I issued warnings,
> you have not accepted correction.
> Acknowledge your guilt,
> Come back, disloyal people,
> follow no longer your stubborn hearts.
> If you are faithful to God,
> the nations will bless themselves by you."

Jeremiah's message found fulfillment in Josiah's religious reforms. Public idolatry was stamped out, worship in the temple purified. It became popular again to seek salvation. Public morality improved. Josiah was charitable toward the poor and needy.

Judged by rigorous standards of perfection, the situation in Judah had its shortcomings, yet compared to life in those days, the Jewish people had achieved a remarkable degree of civilization, wisdom and justice. Still, the country was about to be invaded from the North by the Babylonians of Nebuchadnezzar II. Jeremiah prophesied impending disaster:

> "The destroyer of nations is on his way,
> to reduce the land to a desert;
> your towns will be in ruins.
> I look to the earth and see a formless waste;
> the heavens, and their light is gone.
> I see no human beings at all,
> the very birds in the sky have fled;
> the wooded country is wilderness,
> the whole land will be laid waste."
> "I, God, give each what your actions deserve.
> Mercilessly, I will destroy you.
> And if you ask: Where shall we go?
> the answer is simple:

> *Those destined for the plague, to the plague;*
> *Those for the sword, to the sword;*
> *Those for famine, to famine;*
> *Those for captivity, into captivity.*
> *I am tired of relenting.*
> *Your wealth and treasures,*
> *I will hand over to plunder,*
> *as payment for your sins.*
> *I will make Jerusalem a derision;*
> *every passer-by will be appalled by it.*
> *I will make them eat the flesh of their own sons and daughters."*

With such visions of desolation, the prophet was hard put to explain to himself and fellow-citizens, why the future would be so grim. A just God does not impose destruction and exile upon a righteous people, so the evils of the people needed to be exaggerated. Jeremiah thundered:

> *"If God could find a single person*
> *who does right and seeks the truth,*
> *The Holy One would pardon Judah.*
> *Yet people have eyes and do not see,*
> *ears and do not hear.*
> *The nation has a rebellious heart.*
> *Your sins deprived you of divine favor.*
> *Terror grips me.*
> *Everyone is out for dishonest gain,*
> *prophet no less than priest.*
> *All practice fraud and corruption.*
> *Amid the survivors of this wicked race,*
> *death will seem preferable to life."*
> *and God spoke:*
> *"The Temple that bears my name*
> *has become a robber's den.*
> *Because they have forsaken my Law,*
> *I shall scatter them throughout the nations*
> *and pursue them with the sword,*
> *until I have exterminated them."*

Jeremiah, as a mouthpiece of God's wrath, was unpopular, perceived by many as a traitor. Indeed, the prophet did not only foretell doom, he made practical suggestions that undercut Jerusalem and Judah: "The nation that bends its neck to the yoke of the king of Babylon will be saved. Those who resist will be banished from the soil and perish." He encouraged the defenders to surrender. For such defeatism, Jeremiah was imprisoned and almost lost his life. On one occasion, the Babylonian army commander who conquered Jerusalem, released him from the dungeon where he had been placed by his own people.

Despite appearances, Jeremiah's patriotism is not in question, merely his judgment. He had raved against Judah, believing that he was expressing the will of God. Once his dire predictions had come to pass, Jeremiah became a staunch believer in return from captivity. The Babylonians were about to be conquered by the Persian Empire. With the same tenacity that Jeremiah had foretold doom, he now became a prophet of hope. Through him God spoke:

> "I make Babylon pay
> for all the wrongs they have done to Zion.
> The city shall be rebuilt on its ruins.
> I will rescue you from distant countries,
> and your descendants from their captivity.
> I will bring you back from the land of the North
> and gather you from the far ends of earth.
> There is hope for your descendants,
> your people will come home to their own lands.
> As I once watched them to tear up and knock down,
> I shall now help to build and plant.
> I am going to restore your fortunes.
> I will change mourning into gladness,
> comfort you and give joy."

5.
Ezekiel: In The Valley Of Dry Bones And Exile

Ezekiel lived prior to and during the years of Babylonian captivity. He felt inspired and was possessed by his prophecies. The prophet saw himself as a sentry to the House of Israel. If a watchman does not sound the alarm in times of peril, he is guilty of complicity. Ezekiel foretold the fall of Jerusalem and exile in Babylon, saw them as expressions of God's vengeance for Israel's massive sins. Through Ezekiel, God also warned of furious punishment upon other nations like the Philistines. Desolation is to be Egypt's fate. Tyre will not hear the sound of harps anymore and become a prey to conquest.

Ezekiel's faith in the future of Israel was affirmed in his deeply experienced, unusual vision:

"God set me down in the middle of a valley where I walked up and down amid vast quantities of dried bones." The Eternal One said to me: "Son of Humanity, can these bones live?" I responded: "You know." God continued: "Prophesy over the ossuary. Say: 'Dry bones, as you put on sinews and flesh, the spirit of life will enter you.'"

Ezekiel did as instructed. There was a sound of clattering, the bones joined together. "I looked again and saw a huge crowd of people, the whole House of Israel, singing." God said, "I mean to raise you from the graveyard of exile and lead you back to the soil of Israel. I shall fill you with the holy spirit of freedom, living once more on your own land. You will be one nation and kingdom. I will renew my covenant with you. I will be your God and you will be my people. My Temple will stand in your midst and peace will be your blessing."

6.
Amos: Let Justice Flow Like Water

Amos was a simple shepherd from the wilderness of Tekoa. Material prosperity had led many people to be at ease in Zion, without giving attention to moral values or having qualms of conscience over iniquities that existed in and around the promised land.

Speaking for God, Amos prophesied:
"Let justice flow like water,
and integrity as a mighty stream.
I hate, I despise your holidays,
I take no pleasure in your solemn assemblies;
when you offer sacrifices,
I will not accept them, nor listen to singing.
Tyre has forgotten the covenant of brotherhood and sisterhood;
the Philistines enslaved entire nations;
the Ammonites abuse the dignity of women;
the Edomites stifle pity.
In the kingdom of Judah, there is strife,
rather than loving and caring.
In Israel, they sell virtue for silver
and exploit the common people.
What do you expect under such circumstances?
The time is ripe for changing your ways,
or else expect the wrath of God.
Justice will not be mocked,
nor turned into wormwood.
Morality is no empty word,
My heart is heavy when I say:
Repent, for the day of misfortune is near.
I wish I could foretell happiness and fulfillment,
yet what I perceive on the horizon
is houses in ruin, citizens in exile.
Singing will turn to lament,
Feasts to dirges,
dress to sackcloth.
I see a plumbline
by which the people of Israel
will be measured and found wanting.
Your sanctuaries will be razed.
Despite all the hardships and woe,
there will be a saving remnant

to rebuild the deserted cities.
They will plant new gardens.
Once again, peace and justice
will flow like a mighty stream,
and your fortunes will be restored.

7.
Micah: What Does Life Require of Thee?

Micah lived in the eighth century Before the Common Era and was a contemporary of Isaiah, Hosea and Amos. He had the independent spirit of a person who lives on the land.

These were the words which came to Micah:
"Hear, all ye people!
Hearken, o earth, and all that therein is:
the devout have vanished from the land.
The hands of the people are skilled in evil.
The judge renders judgment for a bribe,
the powerful pronounce as they please.
It is difficult to put trust in a neighbor or friend.
Son insults father, daughter defies mother;
the land is desolate.
In these bad times, let us not despair,
for it shall come to pass
that they shall beat their swords into plowshares
and their spears into pruninghooks.
Nation shall not lift up sword against nation,
neither shall they learn war anymore.
Each man will sit under his vine and fig tree,
and none shall make them afraid.
Wherewith shall I come before God
and bow myself before the most High?
Shall I come with burnt offerings?
Will God be pleased with thousands of rams?
Shall I give my firstborn?
What is it that life requires of thee,
but to do justly, love mercy
and walk humbly with thy God?

CHAPTER SEVEN
OF LIFE AND DEATH

Prologue: Perennial Stories

The rich lore of Old Testament stories is an essential part of the Biblical heritage. Still there is a need to update. The traditional ending in the Book of Job, for example, has the aggrieved party repent in dust and ashes, encouraging the attitude of "blaming the victim."

In "Job Answers God," the divine wager with Satan at the expense of a righteous man is not glossed over. Instead of accepting a double standard and surrendering unconditionally before the majesty of the Creator, Job confronts the arbitrary suffering and emerges as God's partner. Authority is not based any more on unquestioning obedience, nor is Job forced into abject submission.

Esther is a courageous woman capable of persuading her Persian husband, King Xerxes, to stop a planned pogrom of the Jews. In the Biblical account, Esther faints in the presence of her husband, inviting compassion and mercy from a position of weakness. In the revised version, the queen speaks from an inner center of strength, overcoming stereotypes of male and female roles. Also, in the original text, once the Jews have been saved from extermination, they proceed to slay seventy-five thousand of their adversaries. Such vengeance models a continuing cycle of destruction.

Ecclesiastes belongs to the wisdom literature of the Bible, yet wisdom is perceived by the author as vanity rather than as a way to deal with the perplexities and difficulties of life. The gentle cynic reacts to the kind of easy morality expressed in the Book of Proverbs where it is written:

"Happy the man who discovers wisdom,
    gaining her is more rewarding than silver,
Her ways are delightful,
    those who cling to her spend happy lives."

Ecclesiastes is against facile optimism and at times goes overboard in the opposite direction: "More bitter than death itself were my experiences with women. Woman's heart is a steel trap and her arms are chains. By God's favor one may escape her; but whomever God disapproves will be caught by her. I have found only one true man in a thousand, and among women, none at all." To repeat such ancient bias against the female sex would only lead to perpetuating past prejudices and present oppression. The conclusion of Ecclesiastes, that all is vanity because in the end we die, calls for more nuance. Much futility and emptiness can be found in human existence. There are also countless experiences aglow with meaning.

The story of Daniel, written between 167 and 164 B.C.E., is the latest book in the Old Testament. It was written in a period when Antiochus Epiphanes rules Palestine. Under his Hellenizing reign, circumcision and sabbath observance were forbidden and the possession of a copy of the Torah was punishable by death. The Temple was given over to the worship of Zeus, something Daniel and his people saw as an abomination. After one thousand years in the promised land, the Jews were at a dead-end. They came as conquerors and ended up conquered. They had survived the hardships of exile, rebuilt the Temple and developed a proud religious tradition, only to be thwarted in the worship of God by a foreign power. The prophets had foretold a restoration of the kingdom of David, yet such a development seemed remote. The earthly struggle became symbolic of a larger apocalyptic contest between God and Satan, Antiochus being the human incarnation of transcendent evil. Daniel resolves the hopeless predicament by projecting salvation into afterlife where those faithful to God will be rewarded, while the wicked will be eternally punished. It is time to envisage a different scenario, where endtime is joy rather than judgment.

1.
Job Answers God

Once upon a time there lived a man just and wise, humble and charitable, who loved God and people. His name was Job. One day, God asked the rebellious angel Satan: "Where have you been?" "Around the earth," came the reply, "roaming about." "Did you notice my servant Job?" God continued, "he is a good and honest man." "Yes but," the adversary replied, "Job does not love you for nothing. You have blessed him with riches. Remove his possessions, I bet he will curse you." "Very well," God said to Satan, "as long as you do not harm Job in person, deal with him at your discretion."

No sooner had this exchange taken place than in quick succession four messengers appeared at Job's house. The first arrival reported: "Marauders have swept down on your oxen, carried them off and killed your servants." The next runner came saying, "Lightning has struck your sheep farm, all the animals and shepherds perished." The third rider shouted: "The Chaldeans made off with your camels." The last messenger could hardly contain himself: "Your seven sons and three daughters were feasting together when suddenly, from the wilderness, a gale sprang up, the house collapsed and everyone is dead."

Job, smitten with grief, fell to the ground, moaning:

*"Naked I came from my mother's womb,
naked I shall return.
God gave and has taken away.
Blessed be the name of God!"*

The Eternal One felt vindicated in his wager: "Job's life continues blameless; in vain you provoked me to ruin him." "Skin for skin!" Satan shot back. "A man will surrender material goods to save his life; attack his bone and flesh, I bet he will curse you to your face." "Very well," God responded, "inasmuch as you spare his life, he is at your mercy."

In a matter of hours, Job's body was covered with loathsome boils. Disfigured, sitting in the ashpit, Job still persisted in being philosophical about it: "If I take happiness from God's hand, must I not take sorrow too?"

The news of all the disasters that had befallen Job came to the ears of his three friends, Eliphaz, Bildad and Zophar who decided to offer consolation. As they approached, they barely recognized him, wept, tore their garments and threw ashes over their heads. They sat there on the ground beside him seven days and nights. In the end, Job broke the silence:

> *May the day perish when I was born,*
> > *and the night that told of a boy conceived.*
> *May that day be darkness, that night dismal.*
> > *Why give light to a man of grief?*
> *I wish I had died newborn.*
> > *My only food is sighs,*
> *Whatever I fear comes true.*
> > *For me there is no peace;*
> *My torments banish rest.*

Eliphaz spoke next:

> *Many another, once you schooled,*
> > *giving strength to feeble hands;*
> *your words set right whoever wavered,*
> > *and strengthened every failing knee.*
> *Now that your turn has come, you lose patience;*
> > *when evil fate appears, you are overwhelmed.*
> *Was any person ever found blameless in the*
> > *presence of God?*
> *Sorrow does not spring out of nowhere.*

It is people who breed trouble for themselves,
   as surely as eagles fly to the height.
Happy indeed the man whom God corrects!
   The hand that hurts is the hand that heals.

Job, antagonized:
   What a friend I have in you;
      I suffer and you lecture me.
   I feel the hurt, where is the healing?
      Is it wrong to think
   that divine punishment should not exceed the sin?
      To lose my possessions is difficult to take,
   yet I can bear the loss.
      To bury innocent lives, my children and shepherds,
   that is too much; my whole being cries out against it.
   I would rather welcome my own death,
   than see my sons and daughters go to their early graves.

Baldad, indignant:
   How dare you question divine justice?
      Can man be in the right against God?

Job, pleading:
   Granted, I am a human being and God is not;
      no suit between the two of us is possible.
   Suppose my cause is fair, what use is my defense?
      The God I sue is judge as well!
   Yet I shall speak, undaunted
      To injure me maliciously
   Cheapens the work of God's hands.

Zophar, explaining:
   When you understand the secrets of divine wisdom,
      all cleverness is put to shame—
   God is no arbitrary tyrant,
      It is for grievous fault,
   that you are called to account.

Job, defensive:
> How many crimes have I committed,
> > what law transgressed?
>
> Have I not wept for all whose life is hard,
> > felt pity for the penniless?
>
> I have helped the poor, when they cried out for
> > justice.
>
> Men and women have a short life,
> yet their fill of sorrow.
> > We blossom and wither, frail like a flower;
>
> fleeting as a shadow.

Eliphaz, annoyed:
> Does a wise man defend himself?
> > You protest too much; a guilty conscience
> > > prompts your words.
>
> Listen to God, forego believing
> > you possess a monopoly of wisdom.

Job, irritated:
> What a plague your need to have the last word!
> > Pious sermons are of little use,
>
> While you speak, my suffering remains.
> > I lived at peace till God shattered me.

Bildad, warning:
> See how passion carries you away,
> > and blinds your judgment!
>
> How hateful you look,
> > When you unleash your anger on the Holy
> > > One!
>
> To accuse God is blasphemy.

Job, furious:
> Stop tormenting me.
> > Even if I have gone astray
>
> and am in error still,
> > God is my oppressor, who hounds me down,
>
> beyond all reasonable measure.
> > My friends stand aloof;
>
> my relatives avoid me.
> > Those I love best turn against me.

Zophar, concerned:
> *I do not wish to hurt you, merely suggest,*
>> *you are digging yourself deeper into a hole.*
> *Once you were glad at the sight of your gains,*
>> *comfortable when business was thriving:*
> *Forgetting that the sinner's gladness is not meant to last.*

Job, exasperated:
> *Damnation. Have I no reason to be upset?*
>> *You claim the righteous find their just reward,*
> *While the evildoers will be punished.*
>> *That is not what I observe,*
> *I see the wicked prosper. I ask; "How come?"*
>> *What is the point of serving God?*
> *What profit do we get from praying?*

Eliphaz, with mildness:
> *If you return, humbly, to your God*
>> *and keep injustice from your tents,*
> *If you reckon gold as dust,*
>> *then God will be your delight again.*
> *Lift your face to Heaven,*
>> *pray and God will hear.*
> *Whatever you undertake will go well,*
>> *and light shine on your path.*

Job, still anxious:
> *If only I knew how to reach God,*
>> *I would travel to the divine habitation,*
>> *set out my case to God,*
> *Heaven would be in contest with an honest man.*
>> *Alas, God cannot be found,*
> *remains invisible, speechless, and deaf.*

Bildad, with emphasis:
> *Nonsense!*
>> *What power and awe is God,*
> *who keeps peace in the heights.*
>> *The Creator spread the north above the void,*
> *and poised the earth on nothingness.*

Job, impatiently:
>That is beside the point,
>>God has ill-treated me,
>was my guardian and became my rod.
>>Who will bring back my sons and daughters, servants and shepherds?
>How did God decide to punish me?
>>Was it a bad joke or a stupid wager?
>Was I delivered into the hands of Satan?
>>I will maintain my innocence to my dying day.
>I take my stand on my integrity.

Eliphaz, Bildad and Zophar having failed to convince Job, Elihu jumps into the fray:
>Divine will does not fit human measure.
>>Why do you rail God for not responding on your terms?
>God speaks by dreams and visions that come in the night.
>The greatness of God exceeds our knowledge.

In the end, God addresses Job out of the whirlwind:
>Where were you when I laid the earth's foundations?
>>Have you grasped the celestial laws,
>or given orders to the morning?
>>Can your voice carry as far as the cloud?

Job, getting out of the ashpit and standing up:
>Dear God, the question that you raise,
>>your supremacy in power,
>is not the issue that divides us.
>>I recognize full well your immense strength.
>Where I disagree is in matters of justice.
>>I did not provoke you through evil deeds or wrong intent,
>yet here I am sick, dispossessed, bereft of my children,
>punished worse than a common criminal.
>I will not flatter you with humble contrition,
>>when my heart is heavy with your iniquity.

I will not pretend that I repent,
  since your actions are capricious.
I have a fantasy that you abandoned me to Satan,
  your fallen angel who delights in torture and deceit.
Is this my foolish imagination,
  or, perchance, the truth?

God:
  Job, my son, since you asked me the question,
    I will give you a straight answer,
  though it pains me to confess.
    Yes, in a moment of weakness, I forgot myself,
  I gave permission to my treacherous angel
    to deal with you according to
      his own desire,
  provided he did not kill you.
    Somehow I let myself be tricked into testing
      your faithfulness.
  I wanted to know, through observation rather than omniscience,
    whether you truly loved me, even in adversity.
  Frankly, I did not foresee,
    the extent of your suffering at the hands of Satan.
  Will you forgive me?

Job, astounded:
  Did my ears hear right? Did Almighty God
    say to me, puny man: "Forgive me"?
  Am I dreaming, is this another cruel hoax?

God, firmly:
  I meant what I said.
    God is not beyond making mistakes.
  Perfection is not of your world or mine.

Job, relieved:
  What a balm on my soul!
    My first comfort since disaster struck.
  I feel released from contending with you.

89

I need not strive for perfection anymore,
and be unhappy in the process,
> constantly judging others, myself and You
by that impossible goal.

God, with humility:
> We have both grown in insight.
> > I was so much in love with my Creation,
> > that whenever anything went wrong,
> > > I took it personally, became incensed and vengeful,
> > meting out harsh punishment in hot anger.
> > Meanwhile you were looking for my perfection,
> > and blaming me for the lack of it.
> > > To be candid, I wonder whether I did not ask for sin:
> > Forbidding Adam and Eve to eat from the tree of life,
> > was it not a way of inviting the Fall?
> > Refusing Cain's sacrifice was apt to lead to murderous resentment.
> > > To make the Jews my chosen people,
> > Set them up for jealousy, revenge and persecution.
> > > I am even unsure about the Ten Commandments.
> > I made them difficult from the outset.
> > > Then I could punish you for your transgressions,
> > and do it with a good conscience,
> > > in the name of righteousness, no less.
> > I almost feel guilty now, but that would be futile.
> > > Let me rather experience the glory of change and growth.
> > If I learn from past shortcomings,
> > > instead of persisting in them to the bitter end,
> > What a way to redeem myself!
> > > A huge load would roll off me, giving up the pretense
> > that from the beginning of times,
> > > I was perfect in wisdom, power and love,
> > while human beings are forever inadequate, sinful bunglers.

*My greatness is not measured by your shortfall.
I will forget about competing with you,
    no more impress you with superior majesty.
Come let us work together, support each other.
    Will you be my partner, equal in dignity?*
Job, relieved, joyful:
    *What a gracious, generous offer!
        In the name of humanity, I accept.
    For men, women and children, to be creators,
        far from being a challenge to you, or rebellious pride,
    does finally fulfill the ancient prophecy
        that we are made in Thy image.
    Alleluia!*
God:
    Amen.

2.
Jonah And The Whale: A Tale Of Forgiveness

God spoke to Jonah: "Go to Nineveh, the great city, and tell them that their wickedness has become known to me." Jonah did not like the mission and decided to go in the opposite direction, to Tarshish in Spain, the end of the then known world. In Joppa he found a ship bound for his destination, and went aboard to get as far away as possible from God's task.

The boat had barely left the harbor, when a violent storm arose and the ship was on the verge of sinking. The sailors took fright, threw unnecessary cargo overboard and prayed to their respective gods. Meanwhile, in the hold of the ship, unaware of the tempest, Jonah had fallen asleep. The boatswain came upon him, shouting: "What do you mean by dozing off? Get up! Call on your god to save us."

Though Jonah complied, the storm did not abate. In despair, the sailors drew lots to check out who might have to be cast into the sea, to lighten the load further and improve the chances of the rest to survive. Jonah was the unlucky one. The crew made a last great effort to row to the shore, yet the surf remained too mountainous. At last, the men decided to throw Jonah overboard, and immediately, as by magic, calm descended upon the ocean.

As the unfortunate passenger was hurled into the sea, a whale opened its mouth and on the crest of onrushing waves, Jonah was swept past the murderous jaws into the belly of the fish. Almost numb with fright, he still had the presence of mind to pray in his distress:

> "You cast me into the abyss, the heart of the sea,
> the darkness of the belly of a whale.
> I am lost from your sight and mercy.
> Save me in my hour of peril,
> that I may look again upon your holy Temple,
> fulfill the mission you assigned me,
> and serve you in every way."

As the fish vomited Jonah onto the shore, a voice was heard: "Go to Nineveh and speak to them as I told you." This time, there was no hesitation. Jonah embarked upon the trip to what, in those days, was the capital of the world, a magnificent city of homes and hanging gardens, center of the arts, seat of a prosperous empire. The shipwrecked sailor, in tattered clothes, arrived at Nineveh, went into the public square and started preaching: "You have built the city upon injustice. Your lust for power exceeds your love of God. Only forty days more and Nineveh is going to be destroyed."

To Jonah's surprise, the people took the message seriously. Instead of being self-righteous about it, they put on sackcloth. The king proclaimed a fast for all men and women. A decree went forth: "Everyone repent, so that God might relent, and the city be saved from destruction."

God, seeing the sincerity of the people, took pity upon the inhabitants and spared them from disaster.

Jonah felt betrayed. He had announced the present wrath and coming retribution of Almighty God and feared he would look foolish on account of false predictions. "That is why I did not want to get involved in the first place and fled to Tarshish. I knew you were a God of tenderness and compassion, slow to anger, rich in graciousness, unwilling to execute a fierce judgment. My honor as a prophet is lost. How will anybody ever believe me again? I might as well be dead."

"I hear your complaint," God replied, "and I do not blame you; I understand your embarrassment. Are you also willing to listen to my side?" Jonah responded with a reluctant, "I guess so," thinking to himself there was really no way out of his unpleasant situation.

"You are entitled to feel good about what you did," God started out. "Had it not been for your message to the inhabitants of Nineveh, they would not have mended their ways. You were so convincing that they went along with your call for repentance. You saved the lives of a hundred and twenty thousand citizens, no mean achievement. You can be proud of yourself. Mission accomplished looks different from what you expected, still the results are far better than the threatened outcome. Be glad for Nineveh's salvation, even as you have cause to rejoice over your own rescue at sea."

3.
Esther: Averting Destruction

It was in the days of Ahasuerus, whose vast Persian Empire stretched from India to Ethiopia. Ahasuerus, better known in history by his Greek name Xerxes, reigned from 485 to 465 B.C.E. In the royal city of Susa, through lavish festivites, he displayed the riches of his domain and the pomp of his court.

In those days, women were treated as chattel. The king kept a harem of concubines, among them Esther, a woman of Israel, descendant of the Jews deported at the time of Exile over one hundred years earlier. Ahasuerus was so enchanted with Esther that, unaware of her Israelite origin, he placed the royal crown on her head, proclaiming her queen.

It came to pass that two of the king's palace guards conspired to assassinate the monarch. Mordecai, a cousin of Esther, foiled the plot by warning the king. In recognition for his loyalty, Mordecai was appointed to a high court office, serving under Vizier Haman, the second most powerful man in the country. However, when a decree went forth that all officials employed at the Chancellery were to prostrate themselves before Haman, Mordecai was mortified, for his Jewish religion reserved such homage to God. A furious Haman decided not only to have his insubordinate official killed, but to take advantage of the opportunity to wipe out all Jews in the Persian Empire.

The Chancellor said to Xerxes:

"There is a certain unassimilated nation scattered in our midst. Their laws are different and they ignore your edicts. It is not in your interest to tolerate them. If it please your Highness to decree their destruction, I am prepared to pay ten thousand talents of silver to the royal treasury."

"Keep the money," the Persian monarch replied, "and you can have the people too; do what you like with them." Accordingly, a letter went out to all provincial governors saying:

"We command that on an appointed day, about two weeks hence, all Jews be destroyed root and branch, by swords of their enemies, without pity or mercy, so that our government may henceforward enjoy perpetual stability and peace."

As the ordinance was made public in every region of the Empire, there was among the Jews much mourning and wailing.

Mordecai had a copy of the edict of extermination given to Esther, imploring her to plead the case of her people before Xerxes.

The queen was not convinced of her ability to bring about redress: "Everyone knows that for a man or woman to approach the king in the inner court without being invited means the death penalty. I have not been summoned to my husband for the last thirty days," to which her cousin replied:

"Do not suppose that because you are in the king's palace, you are going to be the one Jew to escape. If you persist in remaining silent at such a time, deliverance will come to our people from God, but you will perish."

Whereupon Esther sent this message to Mordecai:

"Go and assemble all the Jews now in Susa and fast on my behalf. For my part, I and my maids will keep the same fast, after which I shall go to the king in spite of the law; and if I perish, I perish."

Mordecai did as instructed and prayed:

"It was not arrogance that
prompted my refusal to bow down
before proud Haman.
But I will not place the glory of a man above divine
    majesty,
nor shall I bow down to anyone but you.
And now, dear God,
spare your people!
Tyrants are seeking to destroy
our ancient heritage.
Have mercy on us
and turn our grief into rejoicing."

The queen took off her sumptuous robes. Instead of perfumes, she covered her head with ashes, praying:

"Oh God, come to my help,
for I am alone.
My life is in your hands.
Put persuasive words into my mouth.
You, whose strength prevaileth,
listen to the voice of the desperate,
save us from the actions of the wicked,
and deliver me from fear."

On the third day of penitence and prayer, Esther went into the presence of the king. Though inwardly apprehensive, the queen spoke with sublime assurance:

"I come unannounced with an urgent message,
thousands of people are about to die an innocent death.
This is no time for me to sit in luxurious chambers,
silent, while my people are slaughtered.
You have been asked to condemn a whole nation, indiscriminately:
the proud with the humble,
the infant full of promise,
the youth in love with life,
peasants, prophets and priests,
everybody—including me, your queen."

Xerxes, perplexed:
"I do not understand;
My decree is for a stubborn nation,
that will not bow its head before the majesty of power,
a rebellious people who believe in a different god.
You, Esther, are not that way;
you are part of us, gentle, unlike the Jews."

Esther:
"That is the point,
I too am Jewish!
I confess I kept it a well-guarded secret,
Lest you prejudge me.
You have come to know me now.
We have been king and queen,
friends and lovers.
If you consign my people to massive murder,
you will have to kill me too, and our relationship;
also Mordecai, your faithful servant,
my cousin who saved your life."

The King:
"Say no more, there must be some horrible mistake;
if people like you and Mordecai
belong to the heritage of the Jews,
They cannot be all bad.
There is no time to be lost.
Let me revoke at once the royal decree
and dispatch to every province
a new edict of tolerance.
It is no crime for Jews to observe their own customs,
they are entitled to the same protection of the law."

Esther was overwhelmed with joy. And to commemorate the rescue from extermination, a new holy day was born, Purim, two days of gratitude for the deliverance, a time of feasting to celebrate in every generation how fear and mourning had been turned into gladness and exultation.

4.
Ecclesiastes: Beyond Vanity, Meaning

For everything, there is a season:
a time to be born,
a time to die;
a time for planting,
a time for uprooting;
a time for mourning,
a time for dancing;
a time for silence,
a time for speaking;
a time for struggle,
a time for peaceful harmony.

And yet, "vanity of vanities," says the preacher, "vanity of vanities, all is vanity. For the toil under the heaven, what does a person gain by it? Into the ocean, the rivers flow and still the sea is never filled. A generation goeth, a generation cometh. What was, will be *again. Life is wearisome. There is nothing new under the sun.*

"I thought to myself, I have great learning and wisdom. Even this is vanity and like chasing the wind. The more knowledge, the more problems and sorrow. Yet lack of understanding and ignorance are not the answer either.

"The wise person sees ahead, the fool walks in the dark. No doubt! But one end awaits them both. "The fool's destiny will be my fate too." Much effort and what looks like success comes from jealousy. I despair of all the work I have done in my life.

"I contemplate the oppression committed under the sun: the pain and tears of victims, the powers and cruelty of persecutors. I salute the dead. Happier still are the unborn who have not seen the evils perpetrated here on earth.

"Those who love wealth never have enough profit. Where goods abound, parasites swarm. Ultimately we are subject to time and chance. A man does not know his hour. Like fish caught in the treacherous net, like birds in the snare, so people are overtaken by sudden misfortune. Humans have no advantage over animals. To worship youth alone is vanity. Who knows what is good for people in their lifetime?

> *I say: Enjoy, have your needs met,*
> *be a friend, experience deeply.*
> *The race is not to the swift,*
> *nor the battle to the strong.*
> *Rejoice in every stage of your growth,*
> *whether young or old;*
> *let your senses give you happiness.*
> *Follow the promptings of your soul.*
> *Cast worry from your life,*
> *shield your flesh from hurt,*
> *develop wellness in your whole being.*

Before you return to dust,
be glad you lived and laughed and loved;
if you have invested your life with purpose,
been good to yourself and others;
if for your dwelling on this planet,
it has become a better place,
there is no need to repeat the sad refrain,
that life is pointless and in vain.
Everything is connected and worthwhile;
each person important and full of meaning.
Beyond futility, allow the web of life to unfold its splendor."

5.
Daniel: Endtime—Judgment or Joy

Daniel was not an ordinary prophet. He was interested in more than the tide in human affairs as reflected in the rise and fall of empires. He wanted to know about the final outcome. Were people and nations condemned to make mistakes over and over till the bitter end, or was there some ultimate kingdom of God? Daniel expressed it in the form of a dream:

"I see the wind stir up the great sea and four creatures emerge from the depths, unreal animals rising out of the waters: a lion with eagle's wings; a giant earthworm; a triple-headed snake; a dragon with iron teeth and eyes of fire, trampling everything underfoot. As I watch in fear and trembling, one beast after another drops dead.

While this scene fades away,
I see coming on the clouds of the sky,
bathed in a shaft of light,
flanked by a company of angels,
a resplendent human being,
serene and full of grace."

I ponder the meaning of the vision and I begin to understand:

"The winged lion is power, prestige, majesty and

oppression. He attracts by his strength and repels by his absolute sway. When the lion roars, he forces into submission.

"The earthworm is poverty, pangs of hunger and hard work. The worm wiggles and writhes in subterranean realms, without sunlight or rainbow.

"The snake is despair and defeat. The poisonous animal injects the soul with hopelessness, parches the grass wherever it moves.

"The dragon is destruction, violence and war. When they are unleashed, they consume all the beauties and bounties of creation.

"The vision of the resplendent human being expresses the final advent of freedom, abundance and reconciliation. Long delayed by the beasts in our past, the snake of the garden of Eden, the lions of arbitrary power, the worms of decay and the dragonseeds of war, our destiny will at last come into its own. The direction of the human enterprise is not toward endless suffering in pits of hell and ultimate extinction. There will be a peaceable kingdom, where none shall be afraid, nor lord it over brothers and sisters. The pains and agonies of the past are not normative for the future. Endtime is not a day of wrath, vengeance and judgment. It will be an age of joy, fulfillment and peace."

CHAPTER EIGHT

EXILE AND RETURN

Prologue: The Road Less Traveled

What happens after prophets like Isaiah and apocalyptic visionary Daniel have spoken? One way to continue is the traditional direction from the four Gospels to the Book of Revelation. This strand of Scripture offers an incomparable wealth of wisdom, insight and beauty.

However, the New Testament has to be dealt with from the perspective of "If the Bible were written today." History has revealed the destructiveness of Christian anti-Semitism, a good deal of which has its origins in the New Testament view that the Jews were Christ-killers. In those days, the crucial contemporary issue of sexism was stuck in prejudice. Peace had not yet become an absolute necessity for human survival. Just as polygamy was common in the times decried by the Torah, so was slavery when the Gospels were written. Much apocalyptic thinking propels us toward self- annihilation, making us sooner than necessary the great, late planet Earth.

The road less traveled and the one chosen here is to see where the destinies of the descendants of Abraham and Sarah lead. These developments, though of great significance, are barely dealt with in the New Testament. The Jewish stations of the cross are marked by heroism, defeat, exile, dispersion, persecution and holocaust.

After Babylonian captivity, the next form of exile was the emigration of Jews from the promised land, a process started under the Greek and Roman Empires.

Life in the diaspora has been a permanent fixture ever since. In 1860, there were only 12,000 Jews living in present-day Israel. Even now, there are many times more Jews living in different parts of the world than in the new Zionist state.

Let us further rcord the extraordinary tenacity and heroism of Jewish resistance to foreign conquest. No situation seemed too desperate for raising the flag of rebellion. Under the Maccabees in the second century Before the Common Era, at the ramparts of Jerusalem, in 70 C.E., three years later at Masada and again with bar Kochba, the courage of the defenders is only equaled by the cruelty of the oppressors. When fierce opposition did not work, Jews changed their attitude, adapting to the host country. Alas, this too often ended in bitter disappointment. No contemporary Bible would be complete without dealing with the searing tragedy and agony of the Holocaust, as symbolized by the satanic gas chambers of Auschwitz. Finally, there is the saga of Return from Exile, a contemporary replay of the Exodus.

What wisdom are we able to glean from these developments? How shall we nurture hope amid tragedy? Are there new ways of directing our energies so that present and future will not continue to be a trail of martyrdom and suffering?

1.
Exile: How Shall We Sing In A Foreign Land?

Babylonian capitivity or Exile was a humiliating blow for the Israelites, now without benefit of country, Temple or self-determination. Jerusalem lay in ruins, the Holy of Holies desecrated and the flower of the people deported. Under the impact of such devastating, long-lasting defeat, a community is apt to disintegrate and disappear from the scene of history, as occurred with Jebusites, Hittites, Ammonites, Edomites, Phoenicians and others in the Middle East. The Ten Tribes of Israel of the Northern Kingdom, con-

quered by the Assyrians, were similarly lost. The Jews of Judah, on the other hand, managed to survive domination by the Babylonians. What made the saga of survival possible?

During the religious reform movement under King Josiah shortly before the beginning of the Exile, the writings of the Book of Deuteronomy were discovered and made into holy scriptures soon to include Genesis, Exodus, Leviticus and Numbers; the Torah or the Five Books of Moses. This gave the Jews a strong religious backbone, a coherent world-view and honorable place in history. Judaism was no more limited to the soil of the homeland and learned to flourish abroad. Jeremiah was first to declare that God could be worshipped wherever sought in sincerity of spirit.

To be sure, many felt deeply the grief and trauma of the uprooted, as expressed in the ballad of the exiles of Psalm one hundred and thirty-seven:

> "Beside the streams of Babylon
> we sat and wept
> at the memory of Zion,
> leaving our harps
> hanging on the poplars.
> We had been asked
> to sing to our captors,
> to entertain those who had carried us off:
> 'Sing,' they said,
> 'some hymns of Zion.'
> How shall we sing God's songs
> in a strange land?
> Jerusalem, if I forget you,
> may my right hand wither;
> may I never speak again
> if I do not count the City of Peace
> the greatest of my joys."

Still, religion adapted itself to the different circumstances of a new environment. In lieu of the Temple as divine dwelling place, the dynamic model of the synagogue was developed and it could follow the people to the ends of the earth. Emphasis shifted from ritualistic sacrifices to ethical religion. The simplicity of prayer became a substitute for animal sacrifice. Judaism emerged from a parochial context to a universal faith where divinity was in charge of creation and all nations.

Despite persecution, the prophetic spirit of hope remained largely unbroken:

> The Holy One will answer the prayers of the abandoned,
> not scorn their petitions.
> Hearing the sighs of the captives,
> God will set free those doomed to die.
> Your sons and daughters will have a permanent home,
> and their descendants be in your presence always.

The Ten Tribes of Israel were absorbed by the Assyrians through assimilation and intermarriage. By contrast, the Babylonian policy kept the vanquished people intact. After the initial shock of forcible deportation, the Jews even learned to prosper in their new surroundings, so that when Persian King Cyrus allowed them to return to Jerusalem and rebuild the Temple, many chose to stay in Mesopotamia.

Yet the expectation that after Exile there would be a triumphant Return is a recurrent theme. Periodically, like after the expulsion from Spain and Portugal, and following the Holocaust of European Jewry, there was a partial homecoming to the promised land, while others preferred to remain in the diaspora.

The first Exile lasted about 70 years and Zedekiah admonished his people in Babylon:

> "Build houses and live in them;
> plant gardens and eat their produce.
> Take spouses and have children,
> multiply and do not decrease.

Where you have been sent into exile,
seek the welfare of the land,
and pray to God on its behalf.
For in its good fortune
you will find your own."

Biblical authors give many reasons for the fall of the Kingdoms, the destruction of Jerusalem and Exile. Among frequent themes are the sins of the parents visited upon later generations, idolatry and moral decay. Two issues seem omitted and are worth pondering. Beyond the realm of what is right or wrong, religious and irreligious, a practical element needs to be considered. The Mideastern fertile crescent is valuable property surrounded by much desert and wilderness, poorly suited for settlement. Naturally, "the land where milk and honey flow" would be coveted. It is strategically located, an important area in the struggle for survival and hegemony. Occupation of this significant piece of real estate made the Israelites into a target for the imperial appetites of other nations.

There is the deeper question of the "chosen people." The Jews perceived their covenant with God as unique, experienced themselves as specially entitled, more so than pagan civilizations. The gift of the promised land was one aspect of God's favor, Palestine a rightful inheritance. Actually, the territory has been disputed for thousands of years and continues to be hotly contested at present by the Palestinians, the descendants of the ancient Philistines. Did the Jews have a divine right to the area they settled after the exodus from Egypt? Joshua overpowered the land of Canaan and thereby seemed to vitiate from the outset God's covenant with Israel to be a peaceful light to the nations. They who conquer by the sword are apt to perish by the sword or get expelled by it. Granted, every tribe and nation has tended to use whatever means necessary to accomplish its goals, among them a desire to live securely on soil they can call their own.

People do not like to be scattered over the earth away from ancestral grounds, rootless strangers among natives. Yet, no matter how justified or sublime the vision, if the methods used to attain it is force of arms, the situation is in danger of becoming flawed. Even victory in war becomes self-destructive. That may be the lesson of how a glorious exodus, on account of a warlike conquest, turned into a dismal exile.

The Israelites are God's people in the sense that they participate in a divinity available to all. The right to develop in freedom and peace is the birthright of every human community. To say that the Jewish people are entitled does not involve special privileges denied to others. Nor does it entail the burden of exile, suffering, estrangement. The Jews, like all others, have the inalienable right to feeling safe in their uniqueness, and to living up to their highest ideals of liberty and justice. Exile is more than a geographic concept. At a profound level, it is a symbol for alienation from oneself when body, mind and spirit, instead of being a harmonious unity, are split off and at odds. To be comfortable with oneself, on friendly terms with nature and the human environment, means returning to the source. Conquest and exile are part of a reality and world-view that belong to the past. Cooperation and being-at-home, rooted in self-respect and mutual acceptance, are ways to enjoy the present and build a better future.

2.
There Shall Not Be Another Masada

After return from exile and the rebuilding of the Temple in the 6th and 5th century B.C.E., the political fortunes of the Israelites ebbed and flowed. The Jews, when liberated from Babylonian captivity, became vassals of the Persian Empire which, in time, turned oppressive. When the Persians were decisively defeated by Alexander the Great in 333 B.C.E., the Jews at first welcomed the Greeks. The period of good feelings was short-lived. During the reign of Antiochus Epiphanes, the fate of Judaism was a heavy-handed persecution, causing the Israelites to rebel under the heroic leadership of five brothers, the Maccabees. In the course of a quarter of a century of warfare, all the siblings except Simon were killed in battle; but, in the end, the Jews prevailed, establishing a new Hasmonean Kingdom of Judah in 147 B.C.E.

Situated at the crossroads where empires clash, and suffering internal divisions, the new kingdom did not long endure. The rising star of Rome and the conquests of General Pompey brought autonomy to an end in 63 B.C.E. and made the country into a Roman province, renamed Judea. These latest rulers were once more insensitive to the fierce spirit of independence of Jewish religion and nationhood. The legionnaires flaunted their power by committing atrocities. Procurator Florus humiliated the Jews by seizing the vestments of their High Priest and otherwise violated the faith through provocative actions. A hundred years after having been subdued, the country erupted in open rebellion. Max Dimont, in his book "Jews, God and History" describes the uprising and its suppression.[1]

"Alexander the Great had used 32,000 men to carve out his vast empire. Caesar had fewer than 25,000 legionnaires with which to conquer Gaul and invade Britain. Hannibal had no more than 50,000 soldiers when he crossed the Alps to defeat the Romans. Titus was forced to use 80,000 soldiers to vanquish the beleaguered Jews in Jerusalem, defended by no more than 23,400 Jewish soldiers. Even so, he was loath to risk the flower of the Roman military in a direct attack, fearing great losses. Instead, he decided upon psychological warfare to frighten the Jews into surrender. He commanded his soldiers to dress in full battle uniform, then staged a military parade around the walls of Jerusalem in an awesome display of Roman might. Earth and heaven were swept together into one immense dust cloud and the blood-soaked

ground shook as 70,000 foot soldiers marched, 10,000 cavalry rode and thousands of battering rams were drawn by the gates of Jerusalem. The parade lasted three days. When the show was over, the performers got a loud Bronx cheer from the watching Jews on the ramparts.

"Enraged, Titus ordered an attack. For two weeks siege guns hurled rocks as big as Volkswagens at the northern walls of Jerusalem, tearing a gaping hole in the fortifications. Through this hole streamed the legionnaires and to the defense ran the Jews. It was man-to-man combat, sword against sword, spear against spear, desperation against desperation. After two weeks savage hand-to-hand fighting, the Jews drove the Romans out. Titus now realized that he would not win in open combat, that he had to starve the Jews until they were so weakened that further resistance would be impossible. To make sure that no food or water supply would reach the city from the outside, Titus completely sealed off Jerusalem with a wall of earth as high as the ramparts around Jerusalem itself. Anyone not a Roman soldier caught in this vast dry moat was crucified on the top of the earthen wall in sight of the Jews inside the city. It was not uncommon for as many as five hundred people a day to be so executed. The air was redolent with the stench of rotting flesh and rent by the cries of agony of the crucified. But the Jews held out for still another year, the fourth year of the war. The end was inevitable. With battering rams and portable bridges, the Romans stormed the walls of Jerusalem. Like termites they spilled into the city, slaughtering a populace reduced to helplessness by starvation. Four years of bitter defeats at the hands of the Jews had made mockery of the vaunted invincibility of the Roman legions, and only killing could now soothe their bruised vanity. The Temple was put to the torch, infants thrown into the flames, women raped, priests massacred. Survivors of the carnage were earmarked for the triumphal procession to be held in Rome, sold as slaves, held for the wild beasts in the arenas or saved to be thrown off the Tarpeian Rock in Rome for amusement. At no time did the Romans more justly earn the grim words of their own historian, Tacitus, who said, 'They make a desolation and call it peace.' Altogether, Tacitus estimates 600,000 defenseless Jewish civilians were slain in the aftermath of the siege."

Under such conditions of ultimate degradation and defeat, it would have been reasonable to assume that the Jews were finally pressed into complete submission. Yet, they rose again at Masada, the desert fortress built by Herod near the Dead Sea. In a surprise attack, they overpowered the Roman garrison and held out against vastly superior troops for three years, a saga of heroism that culminated in this oration by El'azar, the commander of the defenders of Masada, altogether 967 men, women and children.

"My loyal followers, long ago we resolved to serve neither the Romans nor anyone but God, who is the supreme judge, ruler and friend of the human race. The time has come that bids us prove our determination by our deeds. Hitherto we have never submitted to slavery; we must not choose it now. If we fall alive into the hands of the Romans, we would be doomed to serfdom. We were the first to revolt and shall be the last to break off the struggle. God has given us this privilege, that we can die nobly as free people, unlike others who are unexpectedly defeated and taken prisoners. At day-break, our ability to resist will end and we can choose an honorable death with our loved ones. This our enemies cannot prevent

"May our wives die unabused, our children without knowledge of slavery. Let our possessions and the whole fortress go up in flames: it will be a bitter blow to the Romans to find our persons beyond their reach and nothing left for them to loot. One thing only let us spare—our store of food: it will bear witness to the fact that we perished not through want, but because we chose death rather than slavery.

"If only we had all died before seeing the Sacred City utterly destroyed by enemy hands, the Holy Sanctuary so impiously uprooted! But since an honorable ambition deluded us into thinking that perhaps we could succeed, let us choose death with honor, the kindest thing we can do for ourselves while it is still possible to show ourselves any kindness. After all, we were born to die: this even the luckiest must face. But outrage, unfreedom and the sight of our wives led away to shame with our children—these are not evils to which human beings are subject by the laws of nature: we undergo them through our cowardice. Proud of our courage, we revolted from Rome. Now, in the final stages, they have offered to spare our lives, and we have turned the offer down. Is anyone too blind to see how cruel they would be if they take us alive? Pity the young whose bodies are strong enough to survive prolonged torture; pity the not-so-young whose old frames would break under such ill-usage. A man might see his wife violently carried off; he might hear the voice of his child crying "Daddy" when his own hands are fettered. Come! While our hands are free and can hold a sword, let them do a noble service! Let us die unenslaved by our enemies and leave this world as free men in company with our wives and children."

After the capture of Jerusalem and Masada, life must have seemed hopeless, yet in 132 C.E., under the inspired leadership of bar Kochba—meaning son of a star—another revolt broke out. For two years, the Jews were victorious in battle until the Roman legions of Severus engaged in total war, scorching the earth and killing without hesitation combatant and noncombatant alike, adults and children, humans and animals. In the end, the Jews were driven to surrender. To culminate the massacre, the Romans tortured bar Kochba to death.

In Israel today, across the chasm of almost two millenia, there is a saying, "Masada shall never fall again." It expresses the legitimate horror of utter defeat, *the desire to be strong enough to overcome the threat of destruction. There is an implication though that there might be other Masadas, desperate situations, except that this time the defenses would not be breached. In a sense, the rebellion of the Warsaw ghetto against the Nazi oppressors was already a modern-day reenactment of the ancient tragedy. Israel, as a country, could conceivably become a massive Masada, two to three million Jews surrounded by a hundred million Arabs. It is an ominous situation when conflicts are survival issues. Every nation and religion is entitled to live, prosper and worship according to its own genius.*

Building better, stronger defenses than were available to Jerusalem, Masada, bar Kochba or the Warsaw ghetto is not the final answer. The basic question is to provide spiritual and material foundations for human communities to live side by side without a desire for mutual annihilation. Let us learn not to develop situations that are likely to deteriorate into an all-out confrontation. May it be part of the divine-human covenant: "There shall not be another Masada."

3.
Two Millenia Of Persecutions: What Next?

Why have the Jews been persecuted throughout the centuries? The ancient Greeks resented the unwillingness of the Israelites to be Hellenized. Antiochus Epiphanes, ruler of Syria and Mesopotamia, accused the Jews:

> "You are the only people
> that refuses to associate with other nations.
> You deem yourself above every civilization,
> are opposed to marriage with those not your kind
> and eat unlike the rest of us.
> I am angry at your proud airs
> and despise your exclusive traditions.
> Henceforth, the Torah is outlawed.

*Believe with us in the unity of humankind;
I will not tolerate your separateness any more."*

The Maccabees rose against Greek domination, saying:

*"We are the people of the book.
Respect our sacred heritage,
the right to be ourselves,
to worship only one God.
Others, in order to survive, adapt to victors,
submit and choose the melting pot.
We wish to maintain our identity.
Do not interfere with our ways,
or else we will rebel."*

Indeed, after 25 years of struggle, the Maccabees succeeded in their revolt. This did not endear them to the Greeks. Many Hellenic authors of antiquity railed against the Jews.

*"Descendants of a mob of lepers,
you claim to have left Egypt to escape slavery.
If the truth be known,
you were cast out from the land of the pharaohs,
because you are unclean,
prone to disease,
a danger to neighbors.
During the Sabbath you sacrifice human beings."*

In those days, Hillel, a great Jewish teacher, responded:

"Our religion is simple:
Love peace and all creatures.
What is hateful to you,
do not do to your neighbor.
That is the whole Torah,
the rest is commentary.
As to the Sabbath,
it is joy, holiness and rest."

When the Roman Empire, which succeeded the Greek, went into decline under insane rulers like Nero, the Romans projected their own degeneracy upon the Jews, charging them with being a breeding ground for decay.

In that spirit, Emperor Caligula spoke:

"Like Augustus, I am divine.
To cleanse your religion of corruption,
let my statue be set in the Temple,
and be duly worshipped.
I will breach no disagreement,
nor discord.
Pay homage to me as your God:
That will be the test of your loyalty."
The High Priest replied:
"A human statue in the sanctuary
is idolatry to us,
forbidden by the Ten Commandments.
We shall not suffer disrespect
for what we perceive as holy."

In antiquity, pagan antagonism against the Jews led to diatribes, libels, rioting and rebellion. With the advent of Christianity, the stigma of being Christ-killers was attached to the Jews who were gradually stripped of political and civic rights. Typically, an early Christian might have thundered:

"You did not accept the son of God,
when the Messiah came.
You are Israel according to the flesh,
that God hast cast away.
We are Israel according to the spirit,
and God has transferred his love to us."

In the Gospel of St. John, it is written:

"A child of God
listens to the words of God;
if you refuse to hear,
it is because you are not God's children.

*The devil is your father,
a liar and the father of lies."*

By now, the Jews were forbidden to gain converts for their faith and, in response, they were largely speaking to themselves:

*"We are still waiting for the Messiah.
As long as there is neither peace nor justice,
it is premature for us to believe
that a Savior has come."*

In the Middle Ages, two complicating factors evolved, the Crusades and usury. The expeditions to reconquer the Holy Land whipped up religious fanaticism. The practice of charging interest for lending money was considered dangerous to the eternal salvation of Catholics. It was left to Jews, whose souls were already considered lost and who became resented as exploiters.

Hatred of the unlike is a common phenomenon. The antagonist is made into a demon, especially in times of turmoil and defeat, as the desire for scapegoats appears. When the Black Plague struck Europe, killing one quarter of its inhabitants, the Jews were blamed for it, accused of poisoning the water. From different, apart and alien to being perceived as subhuman and inhuman, it was only a short step.

The idea of the ghetto resulted from the tendency implanted in Christianity from the fourth to fifth centuries to isolate the Jews and humiliate them. The ghetto did not appear as a permanent institution until its introduction in Venice in 1516.

In 1555, Pope Paul IV ordered that the anti-Jewish program of establishing ghettos should be applied in Rome and the Papal States.

The ghetto was accompanied by imposition of the badge, compulsory attendance of Jews at conversionary sermons, restriction of the professions and other humiliations. Generally, the authorities did not *allow extension of the ghetto boundaries, even when the population had increased; the ghettos were, therefore, crowded and unsanitary. For the same reason, additional stories were built onto the existing houses and the buildings were in constant danger of collapse. According to papal decree, when a ghetto was established, it was to have one gate only, guarded by Christian gatekeepers, whose salaries the Jews were compelled to pay; the gates were closed at night and on all important Christian festivals, during which time no Jew was permitted to leave the ghetto.*

The Talmud states:

> *"For the sake of peace among creatures,*
> *The descent of all men and women*
> *is traced back to Adam and Eve,*
> *so that none may say to a neighbor,*
> *my parent is greater than yours."*

Belief in a common ancestry is part of the Christian principle of the equality of all before God. However, medieval society was divided into three estates— commoners, clergy and nobility—superiority being ascribed to the "blue blood" of the latter. As most of Europe's reigning monarchs were of Germanic origin, there was a tendency to accord a measure of preeminence to 'Germanic blood.'

Through the ages, prejudice against the Jews has had a vast array of rationales to justify persecution and discrimination. No matter how fantastic, the accusation of blood libel—Jews drink the blood of Christians for Passover or other rituals—was a popular belief. The "Protocols of the Elders of Zion," which raised the specter of a worldwide Jewish conspiracy aimed at exterminating the Gentiles, though shown to be a forgery, has had a wide circulation and impact.

The massive nature of the anti-semitic assault is amazing and frightening. Antagonism against the Jews spans continents, millenia and diverse social systems: antiquity, the feudal society, capitalism and socialism.

Contributing factors can be found in the realm of religious intolerance, economic competition, jealousy, nationalist fervor and racial prejudice. Especially when these different strands are combined, they have the markings of pogroms, wholesale expulsion and attempted genocide. Are Jews condemned to a tragic fate?

It is important to note that martyrdom is not confined to the Jews. Native Americans, the Irish, the Poles, Blacks and Armenians, to name a few, have suffered inordinately in the course of their history. Along with the six million Jews who died in the holocaust, there were five million non-Jews who encountered a similar fate.

Nor are all members of religious groups unanimous in their rejection of Jews. While some Christians see them as deicides, others honor the contributions of Judaism to the world, appreciate that Jesus was a Jew and see in his crucifixion the work of the Romans. The fact that Pontius Pilate washed his hands in innocence was a self-serving gesture. It must also be seen in the context that the gospels were penned under Roman occupation and with an eye not to provoke its wrath.

Similarly, though Jews and Christians alike are infidels to Moslems, they are also respected for being "the people of the Book," Abraham is accepted as a prophet and some of the flowering of Jewish culture took place in Moslem lands.

A crucial, much-neglected aspect relates to blaming. When events go wrong as, from a German perspective, the loss of World War I, there is a search for a scapegoat on whom to unload one's frustrations. The Jews have been a convenient target. It is important for nations to learn that looking for a culprit is not the answer. Blaming is a way of sidestepping issues, rather than a problem-solving tool. When victims of some natural or social catastrophe turn into persecutors, the cycle of animosity and destruction is maintained.

Another essential insight is an awareness that to be

different or apart is all right. No two individuals are exactly alike, as even fingerprints testify; similarly, no nation or religion is the same. Each has its strengths and weaknesses. The Jews have made highly significant contributions in a large number of fields. At any rate, there is no justification for discrimination or a denial of the right to exist. When a human being has shortcomings, do you attack that person? It seems preferable to give the individual added nurture. Let the same attitude prevail with regard to national and religious communities.

The memories of past hurts are extremely painful. The time is here for Jews, Christians and Moslems to support one another when under stress and to rejoice in each others' achievements. In this way, the chain of mutual recrimination, distrust and enmity shall be replaced by the blessings of goodwill, peace and harmony.

4.
The Mystery And Message Of Auschwitz

The holocaust, in ancient Israelite practice, is a burnt offering to God. How strange that the destruction of five million Jewish men and women and one million children should be called holocaust, as if it were an offering to appease an angry God. After four thousand years of history, with its prophets, judges, freedom fighters, rabbis, philosophers, scientists and artists, their civilization culminated in an unprecedented cataclysm. During the Spanish Inquisition, the Jews still had three choices: conversion to Christianity, expulsion, death. The holocaust reduced those options to one: extermination. The only difference was the manner in which the annihilation would proceed: concentration camps, death marches, firing squad, hunger, suicide, torture or gas chambers. The name of the game was merciless, ultimate genocide.

The holocaust literature from Anne Frank to Victor Frankl is an eloquent testimony to the indomitable human spirit. Elie Wiesel writes about the unspeakable experience:[2]

"Treblinka, Birkenau, Belsen, Buchenwald, Auschwitz, Mauthausen, Majdanek: somber capitals of a strange kingdom, immense and timeless, where Death as sovereign, assumed the face of God.

"To convey the truth of the holocaust it is not enough to have listened to the survivors; one must find a way to add the silence left behind by millions of unknowns. One cannot conceive of the holocaust except as a mystery, begotten by the dead. Auschwitz defies the novelist's language, the historian's analysis, the vision of the prophet.

"Written off and abandoned, no power will grant protection to the Jews. Everything proceeds as though they did not exist. As though Auschwitz were but a peaceful town somewhere in Silesia. President Roosevelt refuses to bomb the railroad tracks leading to it. When consulted, Winston Churchill concurs in the refusal. Moscow condemns German atrocities against civilian populations, but blankets in silence the massacre of the Jews. Spring 1945: emerging from its nightmare, the world discovers the camps, the death factories. The senseless horror, the debasement: the absolute reign of evil. Victory tastes of ashes.

"To be a Jew is to ask a question, a thousand questions, yet always the same—of society, of others, of oneself, of death and of God. Why and how survive in a universe which negates you? Or: How can you reconcile yourself with history and the graves it digs? Or: How should you answer the Jewish child who insists: I don't want to suffer, I no longer want to suffer without knowing why. And then, the big question, the most serious of all: How does one answer the person who demands an interpretation of God's silence at the very moment when man—any man, Jew or non-Jew—has greater need than ever of God's word, let alone God's mercy? Just as one cannot conceive of such slaughter with God, it is inconceivable without God. All explana-

tions fail. The agony of the believer equals the bewilderment of the non-believer. If God is the answer, it must be the wrong answer. There is no answer.

"You too have lived the holocaust. You were born after Auschwitz? No matter. One can step inside the fiery gates twenty-five, fifty years later. Do you know Uri-Zvi Greenberg? The Israeli poet and visionary tells the story of a young Jew in King Herod's time who left Jerusalem for Rome. He had taken along a pillow which remained with him always. One night, as he slept, the pillow caught fire. That very same night, the Temple burst into flames in Jerusalem. Yes, one can live a thousand miles away from the Temple and see it burn. One can die in Auschwitz after Auschwitz."

The holocaust remains forever a scar on the collective conscience of humanity. It expresses a murderous intent, turned into an irreversible act. Cain of old can be understood as a myth, a statement of how a brother has fratricidal feelings. Auschwitz is a reality that happened. Cain can be overcome by substituting a vision of fraternal affection. How can the holocaust be exorcised?

Essential in person-to-person, national and international relationships is a firm, unconditional commitment to a non-violent resolution of conflict. Ethnic and religious communities are often at odds, mutually hateful, lacking in trust and competing for territory or allegiance. Yet, we need to open ourselves to the overwhelming revelation that war is not an option any more. Auschwitz and Hiroshima are solemn symbolic warnings to humankind that violence is obsolete and, in a global holocaust, could eliminate human life on this planet.

Traditionally, the use of force has been considered an expression of strength, courage, even heroism. Let us acknowledge that violence has another face, which spells failure and despair. The Nazi leaders and accomplices, frustrated by defeat in World War I and *economic hardship, projecting their own inadequacy, vented their rage in an orgy of destruction.*

A prejudicial attitude against Jews has existed for two millenia and all along it has produced poisonous fruits of persecution, ghettos and expulsions. Yet, the holocaust's intensity was terrifying. Based on historical precedent, the Jews themselves thought that the fury would somehow abate. Outbursts of hatred come and go, yet this time we see a single-minded, systematic obsession coupled with an explosion of technology, causing a monstrous escalation in destructive impact. What the apocalyptic horrors of the gas chambers were to the descendants of Abraham and Sarah, nuclear and biological weaponry could now become to all the heirs of Adam and Eve. The handwriting is on the wall for those who have eyes to see: the divine-human covenant of peace shall not be denied or delayed. That is the message of Auschwitz.

5.
Return To Israel

From Roman days to the present, the physical link of Jews to Palestine has been tenuous, yet it has endured despite a harrowing combination of massacres, invasions, typhoid fever and discrimination.

After the destruction of Jerusalem in 70 C.E., some three hundred thousand Jews were carried off into bondage for dispersion through the Empire, while only a few thousand managed to survive at home. About a millenium later, Rabbi Gershom wrote this penitential prayer:

"*The Holy city and its countries
are for mockery and plunder,
all her treasures are spoiled and vanished,
nothing remains save the Torah.
If once you were children, beloved and cherished,
now you are cast off like homeless dogs!
Are you not yet convinced that your hope is mad
    vanity?*"

In the 19th century, this lamentation still reflected reality. Jerusalem was desolate. Where milk and honey used to flow, the soil was a wasteland without trees, malaria-infested swamps, rocks and ruins.

In the diaspora, throughout the nineteen hundred years of exile, a deep longing for the Holy Land remained alive. There was never a time when individuals and groups did not defy all obstacles in a desire to return to the land of their ancestors.

Following the ravages wrought by Roman legions, the Jews achieved a modest revival, compiled the Palestine Talmud and by the year 1000 C.E., reached slightly over a quarter of a million souls. With the arrival of the Crusaders shortly thereafter, systematic genocide was practiced again, so that by the year 1169, no more than ten hundred families are believed to have survived. Saladin's Arab conquest of the land and tolerant Moslem regime permitted Jewish pilgrimages to resume, replenishing somewhat the decimated ranks. After an initial period of good will under the Turkish Empire, conditions deteriorated to the point that around the middle of the 19th century, a mere handful of six thousand Jews barely eked out an existence in the holy cities of Jerusalem, Safed, Hebron and Tiberias.

Meanwhile, in Western Europe, with the French Revolution and Enlightenment, a new era seemed to open. The trend was toward equal rights for all citizens, yet there was a price tag attached: Jews were expected to assimilate.

By 1870, religious liberty was officially established in the new German Empire, Austria-Hungary and Rome. Legal emancipation though did not bring acceptance. In Germany, anti-Jewish riots took place in times of economic crisis. In Hungary, blood libel was revived with trumped-up charges that a Christian child had been murdered to use its blood for Jewish rituals. In 1894, Captain Alfred Dreyfus, a member of the French General Staff, accused of betraying military *secrets to the German government, was falsely condemned to a life sentence of imprisonment on Devil's Island. Eventually, the President of France pardoned Dreyfus and the court of appeals proclaimed him innocent; but great damage had already been done, French anti-Semitism sending shock-waves into the nation and beyond.*

Under the impact of this hostile climate, Theodor Herzl, a Viennese journalist of the Jewish faith, became convinced that the best option for the dispersed descendants of Abraham and Sarah was to return to the land of Israel. He wrote "The Jewish State" and founded what became known as the Zionist movement.

> The Jewish people are scattered, stateless,
> persecuted, passive, demoralized
> and sunk in abnormal economic existence.
> They lack a common language,
> are plagued by love of suffering,
> by rationalizing some divine mission
> to explain their vulnerable existence
> and miserable way of life.
> Zionism is going to change all that.
> To the scattered, it offers ingathering;
> to the stateless, a state;
> to the helpless, mastery;
> to the passive, activity.

Actually, Jewish influx into the Holy Land got off to a slow start. From 1882 to 1939, five waves of immigration yielded only four hundred thousand immigrants, less than the increase in the Arab population during the same period.

In Europe after the Second World War, hundreds of thousands of half-starved survivors were packed into displaced persons camps, while the annual quota of immigration to Palestine was set at 18,000. In the eighty-fourth Psalm it is written:

> *"Even the sparrow finds a home,*
> *and the swallow a nest for herself,*
> *where she may lay her young . . ."*

but the Jews had nowhere to lay their heads.

> *"Illegal boats. Illegal Jews.*[3]
> *All ports sealed. All hearts closed.*
> *The drama had lasted too long.*
> *We are tired of apologizing for our existence.*
> *If I should go to Poland or Germany,*
> *every stone, every tree would remind me*
> *of children killed, human beings asphyxiated.*
> *When I go to Israel,*
> *every stone and tree is a reminder of work and glory,*
> *prophets and psalmists, loyalty and holiness.*
> *Jews go to Israel for renewal,*
> *the experience of resurrection."*

Yet, a fundamental unresolved issue cast its ominous shadow over the return to Zion. Just as the Exodus under Moses did not take into account the presence of Canaanites in the promised land, so Zionism proceeded as if there were no Arabs with whom the country would need to be shared. This blind spot in Zionist consciousness was understandable, considering the moral danger in which Jewry found itself. All that seemed to matter was to save Jews from impending holocaust and its aftermath. The question of whether there would be a federated, bi-national State, two separate political entities or some other arrangement, appeared remote and academic.

In 1948, the founding of Israel was an unparalleled historic event. Almost two thousand years after the destruction of the Holy City, Jerusalem the Golden rose from its ashes. Living in the diaspora became optional for Jews who reestablished their ancient national home, free from foreign domination.

However, this momentous development was be-

clouded by the unwillingness of Arab nations to concede the existence of a Jewish State. A fierce eight-month long war ensued, beginning May 15, 1948, one minute after midnight, the day after the Declaration of Independence. The combined armies of Egypt, Syria, Lebanon and Jordan, supported by contingents from Saudi Arabia and Iraq, invaded Israel. Abdul Rahman Assam Pasha, Secretary General of the Arab League, declared: "This will be a war of extermination ... like the Mongol massacres and Crusades."

Events took a different turn, resulting in hundreds of thousands of Palestinian refugees. In the next quarter of a century, three more armed conflicts followed, involving heavy losses. In past history, the assumption was mostly that one group would be the winner, another the loser. In our complex, modern world, the terms are changing. The state of the art requires solutions where cooperation replaces confrontation. It is time to work out a new scenario where Jews and Arabs can both be winners. It is unthinkable, after all, that the trail of persecution and genocide continue, with the novel twist of the Jews being thrown into the sea. It is also inconceivable that Israel can permanently impose a military solution that disregards the Palestinians.

With the accomplished return to Zion, let us remind ourselves of a dominant motif of the original Old Testament: the enmity between brothers. In the ancient version, Cain kills Abel, modeling a fratricidal struggle between two semitic nations. The disagreement that separates Jacob from Esau is around privileges of the first-born or, from a larger perspective, the rights of first settlers against those who came later. Many tragic wars with rivers of blood-shed have been fought over this issue. Finally, the story of Ishmael and Isaac is on the theme: Who is legitimate?

The answer is simple: equality is of the essence. There are neither superior rights nor special privileges. All brothers and sisters are entitled, similarly with na-

tions. Rather than living in a spirit of mutual jealousy and distrust, or even killing each other off the face of the earth, Israelis and Palestinians are called to dwell in harmony, fulfilling the divine covenant of peace.

EPILOGUE
YOU CAN GO HOME AGAIN

According to the original Old Testament story, Adam and Eve started out by living in Paradise and subsequently were expelled from the Garden of Eden. What did the Fall entail? It meant several fateful developments which have affected humankind ever since.

The rise of consciousness and civilization has made living complicated and difficult. To survive, men needed to earn their livelihood by the sweat of their brow. Women are condemned to painful childbirth and have been made inferior to men. God banished Adam and Eve, posting angels with a flashing sword at the gates to guard against any return of the first couple or their descendants. Once outside the charmed circle of the divine habitation, an act of violence occurs. Cain kills his brother Abel.

As we look upon the world today, what do we see? Alas, the ancient curse still appears to be with us and in some ways seems more overwhelming than ever. The earth is ravished by technology. We are polluting the air, soil and water. The whale who saved Jonah's life is in danger of extinction. Humankind is losing touch with nature and the creative flow of life. The world is turning artificial, plastics and asphalt, metropolis and computers. Poverty is widespread; every year, millions die of hunger. The vast majority of people labor hard to survive. The subjection of women is an almost universal condition. Violence exists within families and neighborhoods. Since time immemorial, wars have ravaged human communities. Weapons of destruction are increasingly powerful. For some, the end of the world is at hand.

And yet, there are hopeful signs and symbols. There is the environmental movement, committed to bring about a healthy balance between nature and humanity. There is a rising awareness that human beings do not stand above nature, they are part of it. When we harm our environment, we are hurting our very substance.

Childbirth without tension and pain is coming within our reach. Women's liberation and consciousness is beginning to reclaim the essential, unconditional dignity of the female sex. Age-old disabilities and oppression imposed upon the descendants of Eve are no more taken for granted. Men are awakening to realize that it takes equality for true friendship and intimacy to develop.

Modern technologies are capable of replacing backbreaking toil. Work can be joyful.

There are new emerging insights into the nature of violence. The world is not condemned to a cycle of warfare, like the change of the seasons. Disagreements and frustrations will always arise, but we can devise problem-solving methods, so that conflicts do not erupt into violence and war.

The amazing saga of Jews returning to the land of Israel is symbolic of the capacity of humankind to make a new beginning. There is nothing irreversible to the story of the Fall. A god of infinite mercy and love will remove the flashing sword. Paradise is ours to re-enter, ours to regain.